Jordan

Jordan

BY PATRICIA K. KUMMER

Enchantment of the World
Second Series

Children's Press®

A Division of Scholastic Inc.

NEW YORK TORONTO LONDON AUCKLAND SYDNEY
MEXICO CITY NEW DELHI HONG KONG
DANBURY, CONNECTICUT

Frontispiece: Trekking through Wadi Rum

Consultant: Peter Sluglett, Professor of Middle Eastern History, University of Utah, Salt Lake City

Please note: All statistics are as up-to-date as possible at the time of publication.

Book production by Herman Adler Design

Acknowledgments

I would like to thank the staffs of the Jordan Tourism Board North America and the Jordan Information Bureau in the United States for sending me up-to-date statistics, as well as information about Jordan's currency and education system. My thanks are also extended to Renata Marroum, Razan Yaghmour, and Ayman Goussous for providing details about daily life and the cost of goods and services in Jordan. In addition, I extend special thanks to the staff of the Lisle (Illinois) Library District for quickly obtaining books and videos that greatly assisted my research.

Contents

Olive trees

Circassian dancers

CHAPTER ONE

The Hashemite Kingdom

JUNE 9, 1999, WAS A DAY OF JOY AND CELEBRATION IN JORDAN. The streets of Amman, Jordan's capital, were decorated with Jordanian flags and pictures of King Abdullah II and his wife, Queen Rania. Crowds lined the route of the royal motorcade that wound through downtown Amman to the Raghadan Palace. The young king and his beautiful wife were on their way to the palace's Throne Hall. There, Abdullah would ascend to the throne, becoming the fourth king of the Hashemite Kingdom of Jordan.

Opposite: **It took a hundred years for the Nabateans to carve this building, called the Treasury, into the rock at Petra.**

King Abdullah II and Queen Rania wave to the crowd as they pass through the streets on the day he ascended to the throne.

Who Are the Hashemites?

Jordan's royal family traces it roots back to Muhammad (570–632), the founder of the religion of Islam. The name *Hashemite* is taken from the Bani Hashem, the tribe into which Muhammad was born. The Jordanian Hashemites originally came from what is now Saudi Arabia. Under the Ottomans, they were rulers of the Hejaz, and guardians of the Islamic holy cities of Mecca and Medina. During World War I (1914–1918), the Hashemites helped the British end the Ottoman Empire. As a result, three members of the Hashemite family became rulers in Jordan, Iraq, and the Hejaz. The Hashemite kingdom of the Hejaz was absorbed into Saudi Arabia in 1925, and the Iraqi monarchy was overthrown in 1958. Today, Jordan is the only country that continues to be ruled by the Hashemite family.

Prince Abdullah (in uniform) stands next to his father, King Hussein, in 1984.

Abdullah had been carrying out the duties of king since his father, King Hussein, died on February 7, 1999. After the three-month mourning period ended, Abdullah became king. Each year for the rest of Abdullah's reign, that day, June 9, will be the national holiday called Enthronement Day.

Jordanians standing along the motorcade route wanted to get a good look at their thirty-seven-year-old king. They knew that as commander of Jordan's Special Forces, Abdullah had performed daring deeds. They also knew that he was a skilled aircraft and helicopter pilot and that he liked to skydive, scuba dive, ride motorcycles, and drive race cars. But they weren't sure what kind of leader he would be for the country.

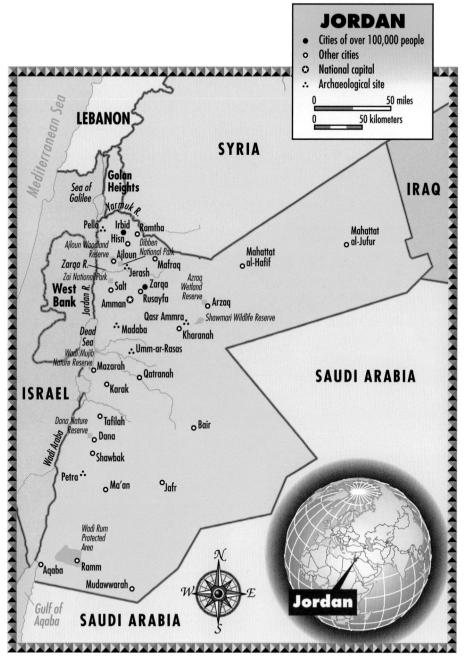

Geopolitical map of Jordan

Abdullah was sworn in as king just four hours after his father died. But the official ceremony wasn't until four months later.

Jordanians weren't the only ones who didn't know Abdullah very well. Leaders of other countries around the world wondered about his leadership abilities. Would he continue to seek peace in the Middle East as his father had? Would Jordan's government become more open and democratic? What would Abdullah do to improve Jordan's economy? Would Jordan's relationships with other countries change? Luckily for Jordan, King Hussein's confidence in Abdullah was well placed, and Abdullah has proved himself up to the challenges of ruling Jordan.

A member of the Israeli border police screams at a Palestinian in Jerusalem. Millions of Palestinians have left Israeli-controlled lands and settled in Jordan.

Peace and Stability

King Abdullah II of Jordan has often remarked that Jordan lives in a rough neighborhood. The neighborhood, of course, is the Middle East, the part of the world where Africa, Asia, and Europe meet. Iraq, Jordan's eastern neighbor, is recovering from two wars. It is also dealing with internal violence as it tries to build a democratic government. To the west, Israel and the Palestinian territories struggle with extremists on both sides who make it difficult for the two to achieve peace. Syria, to the north, is tightly controlled by a dictatorship. Since the 1970s, Lebanon, which lies to the north of Israel, has gone through several civil wars, has been attacked by Israel, and has had its government interfered with by Syria. With the

Opposite: **Jordan has many remarkable ancient sites. The ruins of a two-thousand-year-old Roman city still stand at Jerash, north of Amman.**

withdrawal of Syrian troops in 2005, Lebanon began to get back on its feet as an independent country.

Among the many troubled countries in the Middle East, Jordan stands out as an oasis of peace, stability, and prosperity. In 1994, King Hussein signed a peace treaty with Israel. Since then, Hussein and now Abdullah have worked to bring about peaceful relations between Israel and the Palestinian territories. On the whole, Jordan's economy is improving, even though unemployment remains high and many Jordanians are poor. For many years, Jordan's government has recognized that its people are Jordan's most important resource. Because of this, more students are being educated, which will prepare them for jobs that will help Jordan's economy grow stronger. Abdullah has increased opportunities for women in government, such as seats in the National Assembly and positions in the cabinet of ministers.

Under kings Hussein and Abdullah, Jordan's government has encouraged the preservation of centuries-old historic sites. Many archaeological studies have taken place at Petra, an ancient rose-red city of stone. Jordan's government is also actively working to conserve the natural environment. Nature reserves have been set aside throughout the country. In addition, members of the royal family sponsor programs to encourage traditional Arabic art, crafts, and music. The combination of historic sites, nature reserves, and traditional culture draws visitors from around the world. These visitors, like Jordanians, appreciate Jordan's rich history and culture and its beautiful land.

The Heart of the Middle East

JORDAN, WHICH ONLY GAINED COMPLETE INDEPENDENCE IN 1946, is in the heart of the Middle East. Jordan gets its name from the Jordan River, which today serves as part of Jordan's western border with Israel and the West Bank, an Israeli-occupied territory. Jordan's neighbor to the north is Syria; Iraq lies to the northeast; and Saudi Arabia is to the east and south. To the southwest, the clear, blue waters of the Gulf of Aqaba splash Jordan. This gulf is a branch of the Red Sea.

Jordan covers 35,467 square miles (91,860 square kilometers), making it about the size of the state of Indiana. Compared with some neighboring countries, Jordan is small. Syria is twice as large as Jordan; Iraq is more than four times as large; and Saudi Arabia is about twenty times larger. However, both Israel and Lebanon could fit into Jordan with room to spare. Jordan's land is made up of three main topographic features: the Great Rift Valley, the highland plateau, and the *badia* or desert.

Opposite: **Rocky formations rise abruptly from the scrubby Wadi Rum desert.**

The Jordan River forms part of the border between Jordan and Israel.

Jordan's Geographical Features

Area: 35,467 square miles (91,860 sq km)

Highest Elevation: Jebel Rum, 5,755 feet (1,754 m) above sea level

Lowest Elevation: Shore of the Dead Sea, 1,339 feet (408 m) below sea level, the lowest point on Earth

Longest River: Jordan River, 277 miles (124 km) within Jordan

Largest Lake: Dead Sea, 394 square miles (1,020 sq km)

Longest Shared Border: With Saudi Arabia, 462 miles (744 km)

Greatest Distance North to South: 235 miles (378 km)

Greatest Distance East to West: 225 miles (362 km)

Length of Coastline: 16 miles (26 km) along the Gulf of Aqaba

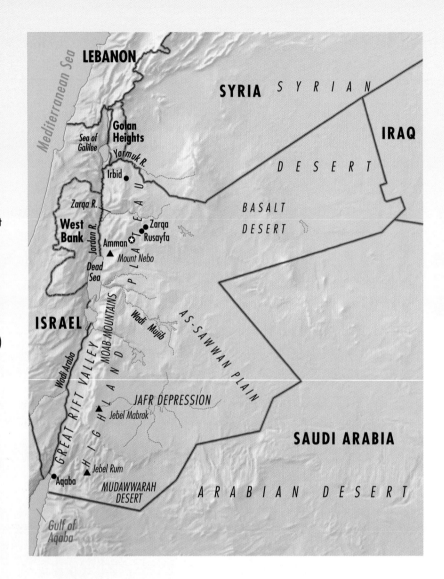

The Great Rift Valley

A narrow strip of Jordan's western land lies in the Great Rift Valley. This valley was formed about thirty million years ago. At that time, Jordan was under water. Then an earthquake

No fish or other large creatures can survive in the Dead Sea, but some tiny bacteria live in its salty waters.

forced the ocean floor up, forming two sets of mountains running north and south. Between the mountains, the land slumped down to form the Great Rift Valley. The valley includes the lowest point on Earth along the Dead Sea.

The Dead Sea: One of a Kind

The Dead Sea got its name because it is so salty that no plants or animals can live in it. In fact, the water is ten times saltier than ocean water. That makes the Dead Sea's water the saltiest on Earth. Because the Dead Sea is in a hot, dry climate, much of its water evaporates. Salt and other minerals are left behind. The thick salt water makes it easy for people to stay afloat. They can read a book or magazine while almost sitting up in the water. Some visitors to the Dead Sea enjoy having their bodies covered with mud from the sea. They believe that the mud has health-giving qualities.

The shoreline of the Dead Sea in Jordan is the lowest point on Earth that is not underwater. It is 1,339 feet (408 meters) below sea level. The sea itself is sinking about 3 feet (1 m) each year and could eventually disappear. Jordan, Israel, and the Palestinian Authority are working together to prevent this from happening.

One plan is to pipe water into the Dead Sea from the Gulf of Aqaba. Currently, the Jordan River is the Dead Sea's main source of water.

The Great Rift Valley extends through Jordan and under the Gulf of Aqaba and the Red Sea into Africa. It then runs through much of eastern Africa.

The Jordan Valley and the Wadi Araba make up the rest of Jordan's Great Rift Valley. The Jordan River has its source in Mount Hebron to the north of Jordan in the Israeli-occupied Golan Heights. In Jordan, the river flows 77 miles (124 km) along the western border and then empties into the Dead Sea. The Jordan River is a major source of water for the country. The Jordan Valley has Jordan's most fertile land, and most of the country's fruits and vegetables are grown there. Warm, humid summers and winter rain make farming possible year-round. Water from the Jordan River is used to irrigate the nearby land. Diverting water to the fields has reduced the river's flow.

Wadi Araba begins south of the Dead Sea. *Wadis* are streambeds or short river valleys. Most of the time, the wadis are dry, but after a rain, water can gush through them. Wadi Araba is best known for the steep, smooth mountains that line its eastern edge. The land elevations vary greatly in the wadi. To the north, the land is 980 feet (300 m) below sea level. Farther south, it reaches 1,165 feet (355 m) above sea level. Then it drops to sea level at Aqaba, the only large city in Jordan's Great Rift Valley.

Aqaba is Jordan's only seaport. It is also a popular vacation spot.

The Highland Plateau

East of the Great Rift Valley, the highland plateau rises sharply. It forms a wedge from Jordan's border with Syria along the Yarmuk River south almost to Aqaba. In the highlands, elevations average about 3,000 feet (900 m) above sea level. The northern highlands receive Jordan's largest yearly rainfalls of about 25 inches (65 centimeters). Because of the more plentiful rainfall, the highlands are Jordan's most heavily forested area. Farming also flourishes there. Wheat is the area's most important crop. In the summer, temperatures range from 64 to 86 degrees Fahrenheit (18 to 30 degrees Celsius). In the winter, they can vary between 40°F and 52°F (4°C and 11°C), but in the northern highlands, snow and frost can occur.

Forests flourish along the Yarmuk River in northern Jordan.

Most of Jordan's large cities are located in the highlands. They include Amman, Irbid, Zarqa, and Karak. The ruins of the ancient cities of Jerash, Madaba, and Petra are also in the highlands. Wadis cut across the plateau east to west. The wadis' water flows into the Jordan River or the Dead Sea. Wadi Mujib is known as the Grand Canyon of Jordan. Winter rains rush through the canyon and over a beautiful waterfall. Another canyon serves as the entryway to the ancient and abandoned city of Petra. *Petra* means "rock" or "stone." The city's buildings were carved by hand out of the canyon's walls.

A river cut into the earth to form Wadi Mujib. Many nature lovers enjoy hiking through the rugged canyon.

The Desert

The rest of Jordan to the east and south of the highland plateau is *badia*, "desert" in Arabic. About 85 percent of Jordan

Black basalt rock is visible throughout the Basalt Desert. Basalt is a volcanic rock that forms when lava cools.

is badia. The Syrian Desert to the north and the Arabian Desert to the south meet in Jordan. Near the border with Syria, the badia is called the Basalt Desert. Its black rocks were formed by volcanoes thousands of years ago. Near the border with Iraq, the badia is made up of a rolling limestone plateau. Grasslands where sheep and goats graze poke up in this area. Some wheat and barley farming also occur there. South of the Basalt Desert, many wadis cut across the badia. There is also an area of wetlands known as the Azraq Oasis.

Jordan's most famous desert area lies far to the south. Known as Wadi Rum, it's really a wide expanse of wavy pink sand. Tall sandstone mesas rise up from the sand in Wadi Rum. Jordan's highest point, Jebel Rum, stands in this desert. *Jebel* means "mountain" or "hill" in Arabic.

Jordan's deserts have a harsh, dry climate. Less than 2 inches (5 cm) of rain falls in these deserts. Summer daytime temperatures can reach 120°F (49°C). Strong, hot winds also blow through the desert. These winds carry sand and grit into homes in Jordan's highland cities.

Looking at Jordan's Cities

Zarqa (below) is Jordan's second-largest city. It is located about 20 miles (32 km) northeast of Amman. As Amman has grown, Zarqa has almost become a suburb of Amman. The town got its start in the 1850s as a village for refugees from the Caucasus region of what is now Russia. Today, it is an important industrial center. Breweries, factories that tan hides for leather products, and Jordan's only oil refinery are all found in Zarqa. In 1991, Zarqa became one of Jordan's university towns with the opening of Hashemite University. Visitors to Zarqa enjoy touring Qasr Shibib, the nearby ruins of an Arab fort.

Irbid is Jordan's third-largest city. It is located about 55 miles (88 km) north of Amman. Roads lead from Irbid into Syria and to the border with Israel. Irbid's population is a mix of Palestinians, Jordanians, and Syrians. At one time, Irbid was a major trading center. Although it still has factories, the city has become

more of a university town. Yarmuk University opened in 1977. Since then, outdoor restaurants and Internet cafés line the sidewalks. They are filled with students, professors, and visitors. The university manages the Museum of Jordanian Heritage. Visitors to Irbid also enjoy the Jordan Natural History Museum.

Jordan's fourth-largest city, Rusayfah, lies between Amman and Zarqa. For many years, Rusayfah was a small farming village. By the end of the 1900s, it had become an industrial center. Today, factories that make fertilizer are Rusayfah's main businesses.

Aqaba (above) is Jordan's fifth-largest city. Located on the Gulf of Aqaba, it is also Jordan's only seaport. People have lived in Aqaba since about 4000 B.C. At one time, it was part of the Roman trade route between Syria and Egypt. Today, Aqaba is Jordan's most important trading center. Besides the port, Aqaba is known for its beautiful beaches and coral reefs. Each year, thousands of people visit Aqaba to enjoy scuba diving, waterskiing, and jet skiing. Other attractions include an aquarium, the Museum of Aqaba Antiquities, and Mameluk Fort.

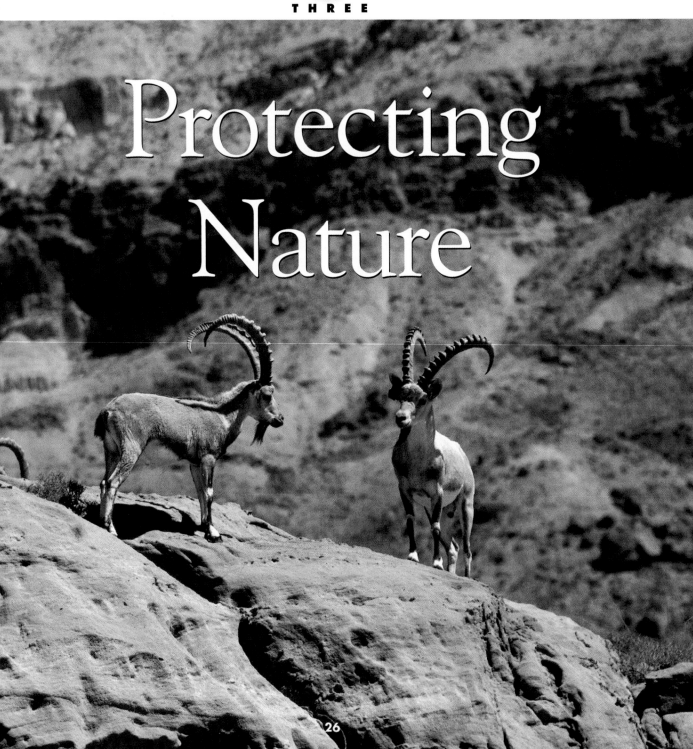

CHAPTER THREE

Protecting Nature

JORDAN RANKS HIGH AMONG THE WORLD'S COUNTRIES IN protecting the environment. The government has programs to improve the air and water quality. It also has programs to preserve Jordan's animal and plant life. A private group called the Royal Society for the Conservation of Nature (RSCN) was founded in 1966 to protect Jordan's wildlife. It was the first group of its kind in any Arab country.

Although Jordan is small, it has a fairly wide variety of plant and animal life. Because Jordan is in the center of the Middle East, many animals travel across its land from Africa, Asia, and Europe. Seeds from African, Asian, and European plants also find their way to Jordan. The seeds are carried by wind and by birds and other animals.

Opposite: **Nubian ibex live in dry mountainous regions such as the Wadi Mujib.**

Queen Noor, King Hussein's widow, has been a leader in working to protect Jordan's natural environment.

Plant Life

Jordan has more than two thousand different kinds of plants. Many of Jordan's plants flower and bloom in the spring. Even the desert is covered with colorful flowers and sprigs of green grasses. However, desert blooms quickly shrivel and die from the extreme heat.

Although many plants grow only in one region of Jordan, some are found throughout the country. Crown anemones bloom with red, white, or lavender flowers. Deep red turban buttercups often grow nearby. Pink asphodels are another

In the spring, wildflowers bloom all across Jordan.

The acacia tree has roots that burrow deep into the ground to suck up water. This allows it to survive in dry regions such as Jordan's Wadi Rum.

plant found throughout Jordan. White broom trees and blue-leaved acacia trees also grow in many places. Some plants are regarded as weeds when they grow in farmers' fields. Gladiolus, deep-rooted Syrian acanthus, and prickly green thistles are a few of Jordan's pesky weeds.

In the Jordan Valley and Dead Sea areas of the Great Rift Valley, willow trees and oleander and tamarisk bushes thrive. The tall Jerusalem thorn tree with orange-yellow flowers also grows in this region. A forest of Phoenician junipers grows south of the Dead Sea. Gray-leaved sage and tar-smelling pitch trefoil grow farther south in the Wadi Araba area. On the wadi's mountainside, Indian sage, cerinthe, and yellow crocuses cling to life.

The Black Iris

Jordan's national flower is called the black iris, although it is actually a dark purple. It grows mainly on the eastern edge of the Jordan Valley and is in bloom during April and May.

Hardy olive trees grow in Gadara, Jordan. Olive trees require a lot of sunlight.

With Jordan's heaviest rainfall, the highland plateau supports the widest variety of plant life. It includes forests of holly oak, Aleppo pine, and cedar trees. Cinnabar, eucalyptus, Judas, and hawthorn trees also grow in the highlands. Olive and pistachio trees are two of Jordan's food-producing trees that grow in the highlands. Flowers, such as pink cyclamen, dark blue hyacinth, light blue lupins, and red sage, add color to the plateau.

Jordan's desert areas also support plant life. Sorrel and pink fagonia sometimes pop up between rocks. Sinai fennel, purple geraniums, and yellow broomrape bloom in the desert as well. One of Jordan's desert shrubs is the spiny astraglus with its pink flowers. Another shrub is the zilla, which has lilac-colored flowers. Wild pistachio trees and some kinds of acacia trees are the few trees that manage to grow in the desert.

Animal Life

More than a thousand different kinds of animals live in or pass through Jordan. Up until the 1940s, Jordan had many more animals. Between the 1940s and 1960s, however, many of Jordan's animals—such as the leopard, Arabian oryx, mountain gazelle, and ostrich—were overhunted. Today, hunting is strictly regulated.

Oryx live in large herds. Baby oryx can run with the herd right after they are born.

Colorful fish thrive among the coral in the Gulf of Aqaba. This makes the gulf a popular spot for divers.

The richest example of Jordan's animal life is found in the Gulf of Aqaba. More than 140 kinds of coral grow in the gulf's colorful coral reef. Coral is a living thing and is considered an animal. Many kinds of fish and other sea animals make their homes in and around the coral reef. Angelfish, clown fish, lionfish, leopard flounder, and lizard fish are only a few of the gulf's many kinds of fishes. The world's biggest fish, the whale shark, also swims in these waters.

More than four hundred different kinds of birds fly through the skies over Jordan. About 150 kinds of birds stay in Jordan year-round. The rest stay awhile as they travel around Europe, Asia, and Africa. Many of them, such as the griffon vulture, Bonelli's eagle, and Hume's tawny owl, use the Great Rift Valley flyway. Pelicans, egrets, terns, and gulls stop at the Azraq wetlands area. Birds that live in the Dead Sea area include sand partridges, Arabian warblers, and several kinds of larks. Jordan's highlands are home to Palestine sunbirds, several kinds of warblers, long-billed pipits, and woodchat shrikes. The sandgrouse is one of Jordan's best-known desert birds.

The griffon vulture feeds solely on dead animals. It will sometimes hiss at other birds that are trying to get at its food.

The Sinai Rosefinch

Jordan's national bird is the Sinai rosefinch. It can sometimes live in wet places, such as the Jordan Valley, Dana Nature Reserve, and Wadi Mujib Reserve. The Sinai rosefinch can also live in the dry, rocky areas of southern Jordan. The Sinai rosefinch was named for Egypt's Sinai Peninsula, where it was first seen. This bird grows to a length of only 6 inches (16 cm). The male Sinai rosefinch is pink, while the female is grayish brown.

At one time, lions, cheetahs, roe deer, Syrian bears, and Addax antelopes roamed Jordan's land. Although these animals are now extinct in Jordan, seventy-seven kinds of mammals can still be found there. Large desert mammals include the Asiatic jackal, desert fox, striped hyena, and wolf. Several small mammals also live in the desert. They include

Both male and female oryx have long straight horns. Oryx use the horns as weapons when they are being attacked.

sand rats, hares, shrews, gerbils, and jerboas. In addition, many kinds of insects, lizards, and poisonous snakes—such as the Palestinian viper and the horned viper—make their homes in the desert. Jordan's highlands provide homes for crested porcupines, ibex, marbled polecats (skunks), stone martens, and wild boars. Families of otters are found in the Azraq wetlands and in some parts of the Jordan Valley.

Jordan is home to fifty-five species of lizards. The blue agama lizard can often be seen near Petra.

Nature Reserves

Currently, Jordan has set aside land for twelve nature reserves. Together, they comprise about 1.5 percent of Jordan's land area. By comparison, neighboring Saudi Arabia has

9 percent of its land in nature reserves, and about 11 percent of land in the United States is protected as national parks, reserves, or forests. Jordan's reserves are under the control of the RSCN.

Jordan's first nature reserve, the Shaumari Wildlife Reserve, was founded in 1975. The 8.5-square-mile (22 sq km) reserve is located in Jordan's northeastern desert. It was created as a safe place to breed the highly endangered Arabian oryx, a type of antelope, which had disappeared from Jordan. Eight oryx from a zoo in the United States and three from Oman were brought to Shaumari in the late 1970s. Twenty years later, the herd numbered more than two hundred. Since then, many oryx have been released into the wild in Jordan, and some have been sent to other Arab countries. Other animals on the brink of extinction have been bred at Shaumari. They include the Persian onager (a wild ass), blue-necked and red-necked ostriches, and a type of gazelle.

Jordan's largest nature reserve is the Wadi Rum Protected Area. More than twenty-five different types of mammals make Wadi Rum their home. They include Asiatic jackals,

Ostriches grow up to 8 feet (2.4 m) tall. Though they can't fly, they can run 45 miles (70 km) per hour.

Wetland in the Desert

The Azraq Wetland Reserve is an oasis in Jordan's northeastern desert, not far from the Shaumari Reserve. *Azraq* means "blue" in Arabic. This wetland got its name from the oasis's blue water. In the 1960s, water covered a great deal of this land. Then the government began pumping water from the underground springs to supply the growing cities of Amman and Irbid. By 1993, Azraq's surface water was virtually gone. With help from other countries, Jordan's government has begun pumping water back into the wetlands. This saved the Azraq killifish, which swims only in the Azraq Wetland Reserve. Before the wetland was protected, just forty-five Azraq killifish remained.

gray wolves, red foxes, hyenas, and Nubian ibex. Wadi Rum is also home to about five thousand Bedouins, desert-dwelling people of the Middle East who traditionally live a nomadic life, moving from place to place. Some of these Bedouins take care of travelers who wish to camp or to ride camels in the reserve.

The Dana Nature Reserve combines nature with Jordan's history and crafts. Many animals live in the reserve's diverse environment, including sand cats, Nubian ibex, and Dorcas gazelles. The reserve also has stone buildings from the 1400s that are being rebuilt. In some of the shops, local people have revived the traditional crafts of making soap, pottery, and silver jewelry. Other shops offer dried fruits and breads.

Ancient Land, Modern Nation

KERAK ARCHAEBLOCKAL
MUSEUM

38

SINCE ANCIENT TIMES, THE LAND THAT IS NOW JORDAN has been a crossroads for armies, traders, and holy men. Armies from Egypt, Biblical Israel, and empires near and far have had the region under their control. Traders from Egypt and India followed routes across what is now Jordan on their way to trade in cities on the Mediterranean Sea. Holy men from three of the world's great religions—Judaism, Christianity, and Islam—spent time in Jordan. Despite its long history, this land did not become a completely independent country until 1946.

Opposite: **The ruins of forts built by Christian Europeans who attacked the region in the 1000s can still be seen in Jordan.**

Many different peoples have passed through Jordan, including the Persians.

Ancient Burial Site

At Bab al-Dhraa, southeast of the Dead Sea, scientists discovered about 20,000 deep shaft tombs. More than 250,000 bodies were buried in those tombs between 2000 B.C. and 1900 B.C.

This ancient tablet is a record of trade between Egypt and the Middle East.

Early People in Jordan

People were living in what is now Jordan at least 150,000 years ago. These early people hunted the large animals that roamed the land. Between 17,000 B.C. and 8000 B.C., people began to build settlements. Remains of buildings have been found at places such as Tabaga in the south and Pella in the north. Between 8000 B.C. and 4000 B.C., people in Jordan started to raise animals and to grow wheat, grapes, and other crops. Some early people began to make useful items such as pottery jars and bowls. They also turned copper from Wadi Araba into ax heads, hooks, and arrowheads.

Between 3200 B.C. and 1900 B.C., great cultures began to develop in the areas surrounding present-day Jordan. Empires grew in Anatolia (now Turkey) to the north and Mesopotamia (now Iraq) to the east. To the south, the united kingdom of Egypt was established. Trade flourished among these great powers, and the trade routes crossed through Jordan. People in Jordan became traders and merchants. At this time, people in the Jordan Valley and plateau lived in large towns. By 2200 B.C., these towns were struggling because of drought and crop failures. During the same time, Amorites—a people from the Syrian Desert—invaded Jordan and destroyed what was left of the towns.

A painting by Gustav Dore from the 1800s shows Abraham traveling into Canaan.

Invasions and Migrations

About 1900 B.C., the Amorites were driven out by the Hyksos from the north. These people introduced horses into Jordan. Some people believe that around this same time, Abraham, the founder of Judaism, passed through Jordan from the north. He crossed the Jordan River into Canaan (now Israel), the land that the Bible says God promised him for his descendants. Between 1900 B.C. and 1200 B.C., trade through Jordan again flourished. The tribal kingdoms of Gilead, Ammon, Moab, and Edom developed in western Jordan.

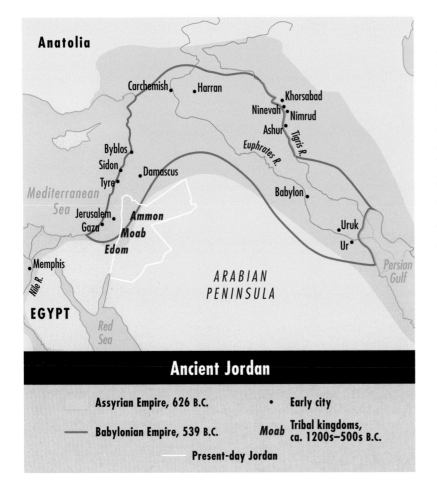

Ancient Jordan

Assyrian Empire, 626 B.C. • Early city

Babylonian Empire, 539 B.C. *Moab* Tribal kingdoms, ca. 1200s–500s B.C.

Present-day Jordan

About 1200 B.C., the Philistines landed on Canaan's Mediterranean coast. It is from these people that Canaan became known as Palestine. The name Palestine for the region of Canaan comes from the word Philistines. The Philistines moved inland and eventually confronted the Israelites. By the late 1000s B.C., the Israelites had come together under King David. From about 1000 B.C. to 965 B.C., David pushed the Philistines back to the coast. He also crossed the Jordan River, conquered the Ammonite Kingdom, and gained control of the trade routes that passed through Amman. David's son, King Solomon, brought Jordan's other kingdoms—Gilead, Moab, and Edom—and their trade routes under Israel's control. After Solomon's death, Israel was divided into two kingdoms.

By the 850s B.C., the kingdoms east of the Jordan River—Ammon, Moab, and Edom—had thrown off Israel's control and were again independent. This independence did not last long. Between 722 B.C. and 539 B.C., Jordan came under the rule of two Mesopotamian empires: first Assyria and then Babylon. Then in 539 B.C., Cyrus the Great of Persia defeated Babylon. For about two hundred years, Jordan was part of the Persian Empire.

Nabateans, Greeks, Romans, and Byzantines

During the 600s and 500s B.C., a group of Arabs known as Nabateans moved into southern Jordan from northwestern Arabia. At first, they raided trade caravans that crossed the desert. By the 300s B.C., the Nabateans had become traders and regulated the trade routes from their capital in Petra. All goods were taxed in that city. From Petra, trade goods were

The Nabateans were making glass bowls more than two thousand years ago.

distributed for transport to cities in Egypt, Arabia, and the western Mediterranean. By 150 B.C., the Nabateans controlled a narrow strip of land along the western edge of Jordan's desert. Eventually, the Nabatean Kingdom stretched from the Hejaz in Arabia to Damascus in Syria. But little by little, first the Greeks and then the Romans chipped away at the Nabateans' land.

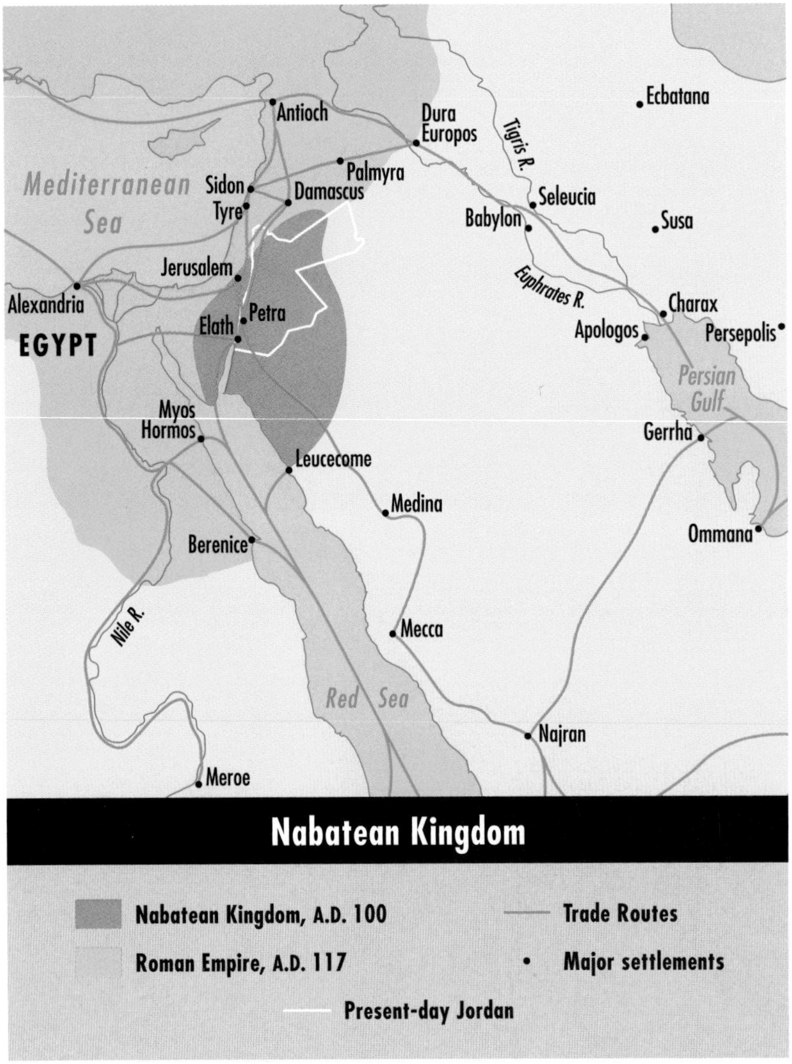

When Alexander the Great conquered the Persian Empire in 332 B.C., the Greeks gained control of Jordan. Under the Greeks, Amman was rebuilt and named Philadelphia. Jerash, Pella, and what is now Umm Qais were also rebuilt. The Greek language and principles of Greek government and law were imposed on most of Jordan. The Nabatean Kingdom remained independent, though the Nabateans used Greek designs in their art, architecture, and pottery.

Nabatean Kingdom

- Nabatean Kingdom, A.D. 100
- Roman Empire, A.D. 117
- Present-day Jordan
- —— Trade Routes
- • Major settlements

In 129, the Romans constructed Hadrian's Arch in Jerash to commemorate the visit of the Emperor Hadrian.

By 64 B.C., Greek control in Jordan and surrounding lands had weakened. The Romans filled the void. The Romans united a group of cities in northern Jordan known as the Decapolis (Ten Cities). These cities paid taxes to the Romans but maintained their independence. In A.D. 106, the Romans gained control of all the Nabatean lands, including Petra. The Romans rebuilt Jordan's cities. Huge amphitheaters and temples to the Romans' gods went up in Amman and Jerash. The Romans also built a wide road from Aqaba through Amman to Bosra and Damascus in Syria, increasing the flow of trade. During Roman rule, Christianity was born in Palestine. The new religion spread to Jordan and other parts of the Roman Empire.

On the floor of the Church of St. George in Madaba is a Byzantine mosaic from the sixth century. The mosaic shows a map of important sites in Christianity.

In A.D. 313, the Roman emperor Constantine declared Christianity the empire's official religion. Eleven years later, he moved the empire's capital from Rome to Constantinople in Byzantium (now Istanbul). Under Byzantine rule, Jordan's Christian population grew. The Byzantine churches, which are often on top of the sites of older Roman temples, are known for their colorful tile floors.

Arab Conquest and Christian Crusades

In the 620s and 630s, Muhammad, a prophet from Mecca in what is now Saudi Arabia, began spreading a new religion called Islam. He united most of the tribes of Arabia under Islam. In 636, the Arabs made their way to the Yarmuk River. There they defeated the Byzantines and gained control of Syria and Jordan.

Muhammad had died in 632. A struggle followed over who would take his place as the Muslim leader. Finally, in 661, Muawiya of the Umayyad family gained control. He established the capital in Damascus, Syria. By the time of Muawiya's death in 680, the Arab Muslim empire reached from present-day Afghanistan to Algeria.

Under the Umayyads, Arabic replaced Aramaic as the spoken language in Jordan. Many people in Jordan converted to Islam, although Christians and Jews were not obliged to do so. Jordan remained important as a trade route between Syria and Arabia.

By 750, the Umayyads had become weak. The Abbasid family gained control of the Muslim Empire and moved the capital to Baghdad, in present-day Iraq. Jordan lost its importance as a trading center. However, its location remained important on the pilgrimage routes to Christian holy sites in Bethlehem and Jerusalem and to the Muslim holy sites in Mecca and Medina.

Between 705 and 715, the Umayyads built a grand mosque in their capital of Damascus. It was the largest mosque of its time.

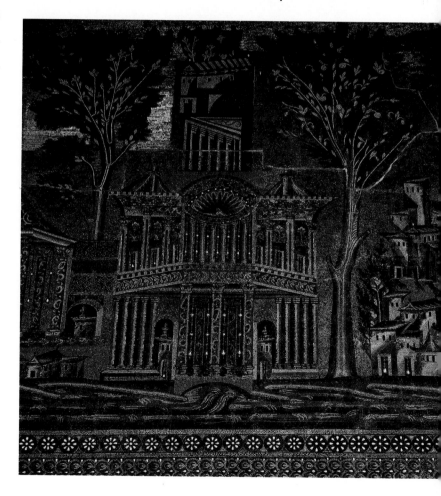

In the late 1000s, the Crusades began. The Crusades were a series of religious wars fought by Christian Europeans for control of holy sites connected to the life of Christ. At first, the Crusaders were successful because the Muslim states were disorganized. In 1099, the Crusaders took Jerusalem, killing almost all the Muslims and Jews in the city. Inland, they captured Muslim forts from southern Turkey to Aqaba. They also built their own forts in Jordan. From the forts, the Crusaders controlled trade and kept the way clear for Christian pilgrims traveling through.

By 1187, Saladin, a Kurd from northeastern Syria, gained control of Egypt. He united Muslims in the surrounding area into an army. Saladin's forces retook Jerusalem and, in 1188, defeated the Crusaders at Karak, in what is now Jordan. Jordan, along with Palestine and Syria, was ruled from Egypt under Saladin's Ayyubid dynasty. The entire area enjoyed peace and prosperity under the Ayyubids.

Mameluks and Ottomans

In 1250, the Mameluks seized power from the Ayyubids. Under Mameluk rule, Jordan again prospered as the guardian of the trade routes and of Muslim pilgrims. Large areas of the Jordan Valley became farmland with the help of irrigation.

Meanwhile, the Ottoman Empire to the north was gaining strength. The Ottomans were descended from people who had migrated from central Asia to Turkey. By 1453, the Ottoman Turks had gained control of Christian Constantinople (now Istanbul). In 1516, the Ottomans swept

into Syria, Palestine, and Jordan. Soon they had conquered Egypt, which gave them control over the holy cities of Mecca and Medina. By the 1560s, Ottoman rule extended from Hungary in Europe to Iraq in the Middle East and to most of North Africa.

Over the next two hundred years, the Ottomans weakened. In the late 1700s, the Ottomans faced attacks from the neighboring empires of Austria-Hungary and Russia. The Ottomans turned to Britain and France for help and accepted money, weapons, and military training from them.

This painting by Panagiotos Zografos shows the Ottomans taking control of Constantinople.

The Arab Revolt

In 1914, World War I broke out. France, Britain, and Russia formed an alliance against Germany and Austria-Hungary. The Ottoman Empire eventually joined Germany in this war. The British encouraged the Hashemite family to lead a revolt against the Ottomans. In return, the British agreed to support Arab independence in the event that the Ottoman Empire collapsed. Sharif Hussein emerged as the leader of the Arabs. Hussein, a direct descendant of Muhammad, was the ruler of Mecca and head of the Hashemite family. On June 16, 1916, Hussein declared war on the Ottomans. He envisioned an independent Arab state that included Syria, Jordan, Palestine, and Arabia.

A year later, Hussein's son Faisal led an army of thirty thousand Arabs with help from British officer T. E. Lawrence, better known as Lawrence of Arabia. In 1917, the Arabs seized Medina and Aqaba. By late summer 1918, the Arabs controlled the Jordanian towns of Ma'an, Shobak, Tafileh, Karak, and Amman. In October, British and Australian troops captured Damascus and installed Faisal as king of Syria. Hussein's other son, Abdullah, remained in Medina.

In November 1918, World War I ended with the defeat of Germany and the Ottomans. Instead of helping the

Arab troops camp during World War I.

From 1921 to 1951, Abdullah was first emir and then king of what is now Jordan.

Arabs establish an independent state, Britain and France carved up much of the Middle East between them. After the war, an international organization called the League of Nations was founded to help promote peace. The League of Nations gave France control of Lebanon and Syria; Britain was given control of Iraq and Palestine.

Independence under Abdullah

In 1920, Abdullah arrived in Ma'an with an army of three thousand followers. The British offered him the title of *emir* (prince) of Transjordan. (*Transjordan* means "across the Jordan," referring to the part of Palestine east of the Jordan River.) At this time, only about 230,000 people lived in Jordan. A small number lived in cities. More lived in villages as farmers. The largest population were the Bedouin nomads. From his capital in Amman, Abdullah was in charge of all internal matters. The British remained in control of Jordan's defense, foreign affairs,

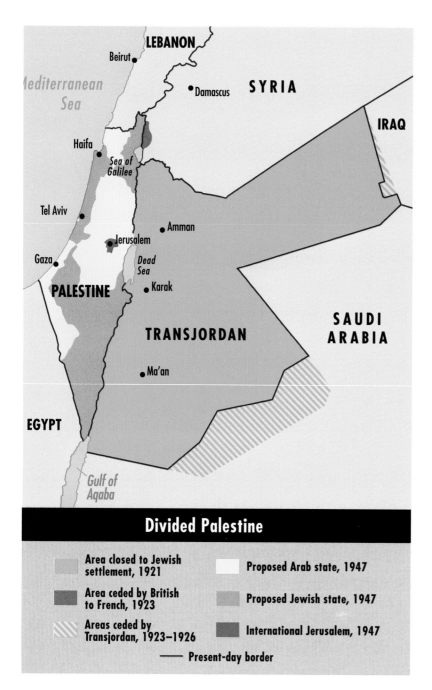

Divided Palestine

- Area closed to Jewish settlement, 1921
- Area ceded by British to French, 1923
- Areas ceded by Transjordan, 1923–1926
- Proposed Arab state, 1947
- Proposed Jewish state, 1947
- International Jerusalem, 1947
- —— Present-day border

and finances. For security, Abdullah set up the Arab Legion of Bedouin troops under British leadership.

Gradually, Britain gave Jordan more self-government. In 1928, Abdullah signed his country's first constitution. In 1934, Jordan set up consulates in other Arab countries. During this time, Abdullah wanted control of Palestine, which lay west of the Jordan River.

From 1939 to 1945, however, Jordan's independence and Palestine's future took a back seat to World War II. During the war, the Arab Legion (formed in 1944 and consisting of Transjordan, Egypt, Yemen, Saudi Arabia, Iraq, Syria, and Lebanon) aided the British. Finally, in 1946,

Jordan gained full independence as the Hashemite Kingdom of Transjordan. As king, Abdullah had a new constitution written. In 1948, the British withdrew from Palestine, and the Jewish state of Israel was founded.

That same year, Arab League countries invaded Israel. When this first Arab-Israeli War ended in 1949, Jordan controlled what is now called the West Bank and eastern Jerusalem. In 1950, Abdullah annexed the West Bank to his kingdom. The country's name was changed to the Hashemite Kingdom of Jordan because the kingdom was now on both sides of the Jordan River. Jordan, which had about 400,000 people before the annexation, gained an additional 500,000 in the West Bank, as well as about 500,000 Palestinian refugees who had fled Israel. The Palestinians were granted Jordanian citizenship and could vote and hold office.

In July 1951, Abdullah was assassinated in Jerusalem by a young Palestinian who thought Abdullah had cooperated too much with the Israelis. Abdullah's son Talal became king, but he soon stepped down because of illness. In 1953, Talal's son Hussein became king after turning eighteen.

King Hussein Builds a Nation

At first, Hussein had problems both within Jordan and with the neighboring countries. Palestinians made up more than half of Jordan's population. They were better educated and had more business experience than the Jordanians. As such, they played a large part in Jordan's economy and wanted a larger say in the government. Some Palestinians even wanted to overthrow the Hashemite monarchy. There were several attempts on Hussein's life. In response, Hussein limited freedom of speech and the press.

Although Jordan still needed British financial aid, neighboring Arab countries wanted Hussein to break his ties with Britain. Egypt and Saudi Arabia promised him financial help if he were to do so. When this aid did not arrive as promised, Hussein turned to the United States. As a result of U.S. aid, Jordan's economy improved. Potash and phosphate mining developed, and an oil refinery was built. The Port of Aqaba opened. Crops grown in the fertile West Bank helped the economy. In addition, many Jordanians and Palestinian-Jordanians moved to Saudi Arabia, Kuwait, and other Gulf states, where they found jobs and sent money home to their families in Jordan.

The PLO set up training camps in Jordan even though the Jordanian government tried to stop PLO activity.

Meanwhile, the Palestine Liberation Organization (PLO) had been formed to work for a homeland in Israel for the Palestinian people. The PLO formed an army of Palestinian refugees, but King Hussein refused to allow them to train in Jordan. He also would not allow the PLO to collect taxes from Palestinians on land controlled by Jordan. Nevertheless, in 1965, the PLO's army led attacks on Israel from Jordan. In return, Israel attacked the West Bank town of Samu in 1966.

In September 1970, fighting broke out between Jordanian and Palestinian forces in Amman. It is estimated that between three and five thousand people died during the ten days of fighting.

Tensions between Israel and the Arab nations, always high, increased in 1967. There were border skirmishes, and then Egypt blocked Israeli ships from passing through the Straits of Tiran, so the ships could not get to the Red Sea and beyond. In June, war broke out between Israel and its Arab neighbors of Jordan, Egypt, and Syria. Israel quickly won what became known as the Six-Day War. In those few days, Israel captured Jordan's West Bank and eastern Jerusalem, Egypt's Gaza Strip, and Syria's Golan Heights. This was a great blow to Jordan's economy. Jordan lost the West Bank's fertile farmland as well as tourist money from the West Bank cities of Jerusalem, Bethlehem, Jericho, and Hebron. Another 200,000 Palestinian refugees, including members of the PLO, entered Jordan.

Many Palestinians wanted to fight Israel, while most Jordanians didn't. In September 1970, which is known as Black September, radical Palestinians called for the overthrow of the monarchy, and there was another attempt on King Hussein's life. Fighting between the Jordanian army and Palestinian forces broke out in Amman. In Irbid, the Palestinians declared their own government. In return, the Jordanian government forced the PLO out of Jordan. When Egypt and Syria attempted to invade Israel in October 1973, Jordan stayed out of it. In 1974, Arab leaders, including King Hussein, agreed that the West Bank should become part of a Palestinian state if Israel gave up its control. Jordan's government, however, continued to pay the salaries of Palestinian teachers and health care workers in the West Bank. When West Bank Palestinians rose up against Israeli control in 1987, King Hussein decided Jordan could not control the Palestinians there. In 1988, he gave up all of Jordan's interests in and claims to the West Bank.

The following year, elections were held in Jordan for the first time since 1967. Little by little, a limited amount of freedom of speech and freedom of the press was restored. The economy was in poor shape, however, and prices were high. Meanwhile, many Palestinians from the West Bank immigrated into Jordan. Then, in 1990, Iraq invaded Kuwait. Thousands of Jordanians and Jordanian-Palestinians fled Kuwait and Iraq and returned to Jordan. These population increases also hurt the economy. Hussein worked to improve the economy, but he also put restrictions on people's rights.

Jordan Under the New King

In 1999, King Hussein died of cancer. His son Abdullah became king. Young King Abdullah II has brought renewed energy to Jordan's government, economy, and foreign relations.

He lifted censorship of newspapers, magazines, and videos. Abdullah also worked for economic reforms to lower unemployment and improve the standard of living. He has brought new investments and businesses to Jordan.

By 2006, Abdullah and his wife, Queen Rania, had become familiar faces throughout the world. The king works to bring more business to Jordan. The queen promotes programs that help to improve the lives of Jordanians.

Women were allowed to vote in a national election for the first time in 1989.

CHAPTER FIVE

The Powers of the King

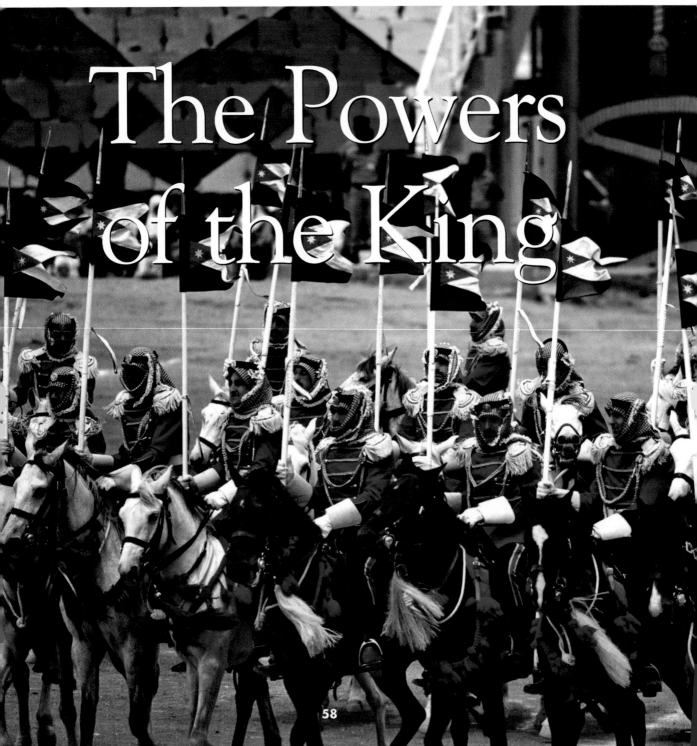

JORDAN IS OFFICIALLY A CONSTITUTIONAL MONARCHY, MEAN-
ing that it has a king but also a constitution that limits the
king's powers. Jordan's constitution provides for three branches
of government—executive, legislative, and judicial. In reality,
however, the king holds most the power. The constitution also
lists the rights of the Jordanian people, such as freedom of the
press, freedom of speech, freedom of religion, and the right to
an education. In times of national crisis, however, the king
can limit freedom of speech or freedom of the press.

Opposite: **Jordanian armed forces on horseback parade near Amman.**

Jordan's National Flag

Jordan's national flag is based on the flag from the 1916 Arab Revolt, when Arabs tried to rid themselves of Ottoman rule and form a unified Arab country. The three stripes stand for the Arab dynasties: black for the Abbasid, white for the Umayyad, and green for the Fatimid. The red triangle represents the Hashemite kingdom. The white star symbolizes the unity of the Jordanian people; the star's seven points symbolize the first seven verses of the Qur'an, the holy book of Islam. The flag was adopted on April 16, 1928.

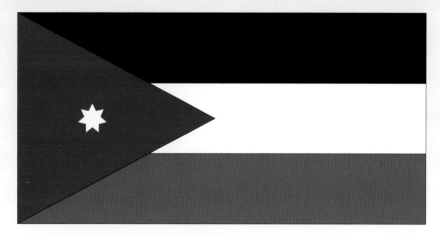

The Structure of Government

Jordan's king is head of state. In addition, all governmental power flows from him to the executive, legislative, and judicial branches. The king is also commander in chief of Jordan's army, navy, and air force. He can declare war; sign peace treaties; order elections to be held; appoint and recall the prime minister, cabinet ministers, and members of the Senate; and approve and carry out the legislature's laws.

King Abdullah II

King Abdullah (left) was born in Amman on January 30, 1962. He was the first son of King Hussein (right) and the first child of his second marriage. Abdullah's mother is Princess Muna. Muna was an Englishwoman, Antoinette Gardiner, the daughter of a British army officer who helped to train the Jordanian army. She took the name Muna, which means "delight" in Arabic, when she converted to Islam and married Hussein in 1961. In 1972, the king divorced Abdullah's mother.

Abdullah's education began in 1966 at the Islamic Educational College in Amman. He was soon sent to St. Edmund's School in Surrey, England, where he completed his elementary school education. He went to middle school at Eaglebrook School and high school at Deerfield Academy, both in Deerfield, Massachusetts. Although he had private lessons in Arabic during his years in England and the United States, he became more comfortable speaking English. Today, he still speaks English more easily than he does Arabic. Abdullah went to college at Sandhurst Royal Military Academy and Oxford University, both in England. In

1984, he returned to Jordan and joined the Jordanian Armed Forces. He quickly rose through the ranks in the army and also served as an attack pilot with Jordan's air force.

Abdullah's queen is Rania Al-Abdullah (1970–), a Palestinian who was born and brought up in Kuwait. Abdullah and Rania married on June 10, 1993. They have four children.

Besides the king, the prime minister and the cabinet of ministers make up the rest of Jordan's executive branch. Jordan's twenty-four ministries oversee such areas as agriculture, Islamic affairs, and foreign relations. Since 1953, Jordan's kings have frequently replaced their prime ministers and reshuffled the cabinet. In 2003, King Abdullah appointed three women as ministers. He also began appointing younger men who were specially trained in their ministry's affairs. In April 2005, King Abdullah appointed Adnan Badran as prime minister. He was supposed to push through plans to decentralize the government and to bring about economic and social reforms. In November 2005, the king appointed a new prime minister, Marouf al-Bakhit, to address special issues of national security in response to terrorist attacks in Jordan.

Jordan's prime ministers seldom stay in the job long. Adnan Badran (right) held the job for just seven months before he was forced to resign in the wake of bombings in Amman.

Jordanian soldiers bring a man suspected of bank fraud to jail. More than five thousand people are serving time in Jordan's prisons.

Jordan's legislative branch is made up of the two-house National Assembly. The Senate, or House of Nobles, has fifty-five members. The king appoints the senators to four-year terms. The senators are retired generals and former prime ministers, ministers, ambassadors, members of the Chamber of Deputies, and judges. The 110 members of the Chamber of Deputies are elected to four-year terms. Both houses of the National Assembly must approve proposals before they are sent to the king to be signed into law. If the king does not approve the proposal, approval by a joint session of the National Assembly can overturn the king's objection.

Jordan's judicial system is also under the king's control. All judges are appointed by the king. Only the king can grant clemency—lessening or removing the punishment for a crime. Also, the king must confirm all death sentences before they can be carried out. All other decisions are made by judges. There is no jury system in Jordan.

Courts of First Instance handle major criminal and civil cases. Lesser criminal and civil cases are heard by the Magistrate Courts. There are two kinds of religious courts: Shari'a Courts for Muslims and Ecclesiastical Courts for Christians. These courts handle such matters as marriage,

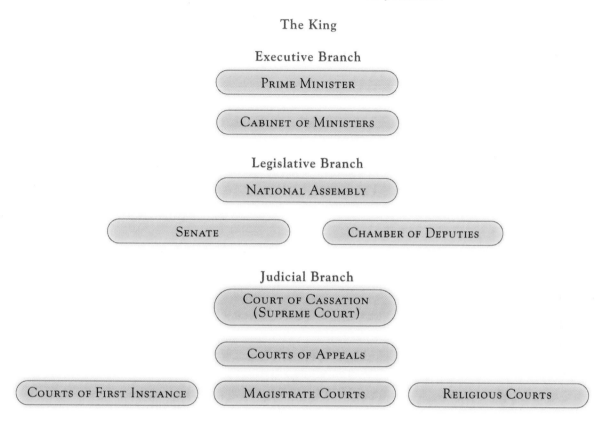

NATIONAL GOVERNMENT OF JORDAN

The King

Executive Branch

PRIME MINISTER

CABINET OF MINISTERS

Legislative Branch

NATIONAL ASSEMBLY

SENATE

CHAMBER OF DEPUTIES

Judicial Branch

COURT OF CASSATION
(SUPREME COURT)

COURTS OF APPEALS

COURTS OF FIRST INSTANCE

MAGISTRATE COURTS

RELIGIOUS COURTS

divorce, and inheritance. Courts of Appeals can review rulings by these lower courts. The highest court in Jordan is called the Court of Cassation. This court has seven judges and a president who serves as the chief justice of Jordan. The Court of Cassation hears cases sent from the Courts of Appeals.

Voting and Political Parties

All Jordanian citizens eighteen years old and older are eligible to vote in all elections. Scheduled elections, however, do not

"Long Live the King"

Jordan's national anthem, "A-Sha-al Maleek" ("Long Live the King"), was adopted in 1946. The words were written by Abdul Mone'm al-Rifai (1917–1985). Qader al-Taneer (1901–1957) wrote the music.

A-Sha al-Malik	Long live the King!
A-Sha al-Malik	Long live the King!
Sa-Mi-yan-ma-qa mu-hu	His position is sublime,
Kha-fi-qa-tin fil ma-ali	His banners waving
a-lam m-hu.	in glory supreme.

always take place. In 1989, the first legislative elections were held since the war with Israel in 1967. Elections were held on schedule in 1993 and 1997. In 2001, King Abdullah closed the legislature and postponed the elections out of fear of unrest. They were finally held in 2003. In that election, for the first time, six seats were set aside for females in the Chamber of Deputies. Minority groups also had seats reserved for them: nine seats for Christians, six for Bedouins, and three for Circassians.

Currently, Jordan has more than ten political parties. The National Constitutional Party (NCP) is the ruling party. It has the majority of seats in the Chamber of Deputies. The Islamic Action Front (IAF) is the main opposition party. In the 2003 election, the NCP won eighty seats in the Chamber of Deputies; the IAF, seventeen seats; the Independent Islamists, five seats; and the Leftist Democratic Party, two seats.

The Military

Jordan's government has maintained a strong military presence. Until 1994, Jordan felt it needed to be able to defend itself against Israel. Uprisings by Palestinians in Jordan also required military strength. Jordan's government spends more than one billion dollars each year for its troops and equipment. All Jordanian men are required to serve two years in the military. Some volunteer at age seventeen. Others wait to be drafted when they are older. The military attracts many young men who are unemployed. It pays well and can become a secure career.

Jordan maintains a large military force. In 2004, the nation spent $1.46 billion on its military.

Foreign Affairs

In 1994, Jordan signed a peace treaty with Israel. Since then, the two countries have had cooperative if not especially cordial relations. They are working on water-sharing programs, cultural exchanges, and tourist programs. Jordan is also working to bring about peace between Israel and the Palestinian Authority. In 2001, Jordan and Syria agreed to build a dam on the Yarmuk River. This will be a source of electrical power for northern Jordan.

Throughout most of its history, Jordan has had good relationships with the United States and Britain. In 2000, Jordan and the United States signed a free trade agreement, which eliminated taxes on trade between the two countries. This was the first such agreement between the United States and an Arab country.

A Rough Neighborhood

King Abdullah II has said that Jordan lives in a rough neighborhood. Proof of this occurred in 2005, when Al Qaeda suicide bombers attacked three hotels in Amman. About sixty people were killed. Most of them were Muslim Jordanians. The attack had been planned by Abu Musab al-Zarqawi, a Jordanian from Zarqa. Zarqawi heads Al Qaeda's terrorist group in Iraq. The attacks were meant to punish Jordan for the king's close relationship with the United States and his work negotiating peace between Israel and the Palestinians.

Amman: Did You Know This?

Jordan's capital city of Amman has a long history. People have lived there since at least 3200 B.C. Long ago, it was the capital city Rabbath Ammon of the Ammonite Kingdom. Later, it was the Egyptian city of Philadelphia. Then the Romans took over. Amman's amphitheater (above) and other ruins date to the Roman period. In the 1870s, Amman developed as a trading center. In 1921, Amman became the capital of the Hashemite Emirate of Transjordan. An earthquake destroyed the city in 1927, but it was rebuilt.

Since the 1940s, Amman's population has grown from twenty thousand to close to two million. More than half its people are Palestinians who fled to Jordan from Israel, the West Bank, and Kuwait. Many of the Palestinians live in refugee camps around the city.

As the country's capital, Amman has many royal palaces, the National Assembly building, the Court of Cassation, and other government offices. The blue-domed King Abdullah Mosque and the black-and-white-checked Abu Darwish Mosque are the most colorful of many mosques in Amman. The Martyr's Memorial and the Military Museum tell the story of the Arab Revolt in 1916. Other important museums include the National Archaeological Museum and the Folklore Museum. The Jordan National Gallery of Fine Art and the Dar al-Funun showcase contemporary Jordanian and other Arab artists.

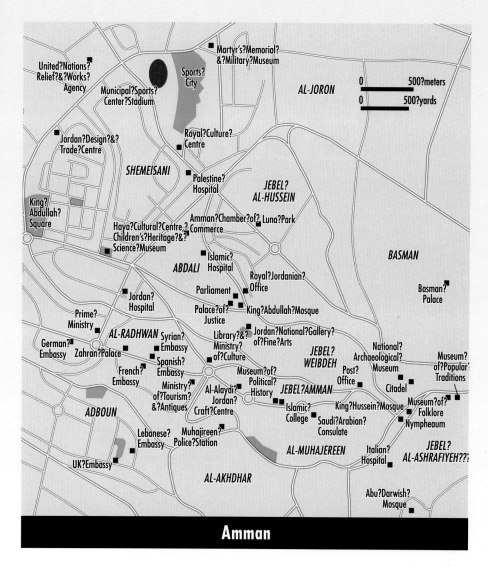

Amman

CHAPTER SIX

Building the Economy

JORDAN HAS FEW NATURAL RESOURCES. MOST OF THE COUNTRY is desert, so only a small percentage of its land supports crops and forests. Few mineral resources lie under the land. Water is a precious commodity. Nevertheless, Jordan enjoys a fairly prosperous economy. Since the 1990s, the government's economic goal has been to maintain growth without prices going up.

In 1996, King Hussein began a program to privatize Jordan's industries. This meant that the government would sell businesses it owned to private companies. Privatization has continued under King Abdullah. Private buyers have purchased Jordan's telecommunication company, the postal

Opposite: **Amman is a mixture of modern skyscrapers and old neighborhoods.**

Jordanians pack a marketplace to buy fruits and vegetables.

system, and the civil aviation authority. From these sales, Jordan's government has received about $1.214 billion. The government uses this money to improve the country's water resources and its health care, welfare, and education programs. Under King Abdullah, the government has also encouraged companies from other countries to build hotels, restaurants, and offices in Jordan. In 2003, those foreign investments totaled $800 million. In addition, many Jordanians who left the country to make their fortunes have returned home to build companies.

Jordan's Coins and Paper Money

The official unit of currency in Jordan is the Jordanian *dinar*, which formerly was divided into one thousand *fils* and is now more commonly divided into one hundred *piastres*. Jordan's coins come in denominations of 10 fils (1 piastre), 50 fils (5 piastres), 100 fils (10 piastres), ¼ dinar (25 piastres), ½ dinar (50 piastres), and 1 dinar. These coins can be circular or octagonal and are made of mixed metals. The front of each coin is engraved with a portrait of either King Hussein or King Abdullah II. Banknotes come in denominations of ½, 1, 5, 10, 20, and 50 dinars. The front of each banknote portrays one of Jordan's rulers. An important event, building, or place in Jordan's history is on the back of each note. In 2006, 1 Jordanian dinar equaled U.S. $1.41 dollars, and U.S. $1 dollar equaled 0.71 dinars.

More than forty thousand people work in Jordan's textile factories. Most are young women who earn just $3.50 a day.

Jordan is considered to be a lower middle-income country. Officially, about 15 percent of Jordan's workforce is unemployed, although unofficial figures place the unemployment rate at about 30 percent. The unemployment rate in the United States is only 6 percent. Currently, about 7 percent of Jordan's workers are employed in agriculture, about 12 percent in manufacturing and mining, and about 81 percent in service industries such as tourism, banking, and health care.

What a Dinar Buys		
Items	Cost in Jordanian Dinars	Cost in U.S. Dollars
T-shirt	5 JD	$7
Pair of jeans	10 JD	$14
Athletic shoes	15 JD	$20
Music CD	1 JD	$1.40
Movie ticket	0.5 to 4 JD	$0.71 to $5.64
Ice cream cone	0.2 to 3 JD	$0.28 to $4.23
Candy bar	0.5 JD	$0.71
Bicycle	80 JD	$113

Vegetables grow well in the irrigated Jordan Valley.

Jordan's System of Weights and Measures

Jordan uses the metric system. However, land is measured in dunum: 1 dunum = 10,760 square feet = 1,000 square meters.

Agriculture

Only about 5 percent of Jordan's land is suitable for farming. The Jordan Valley and the highland plateau are the main farming areas. In the valley, water from the Jordan River is used to irrigate nearby farmland. The main crops are tomatoes, cucumbers, watermelons, cantaloupes, cauliflower, cabbages, lettuce, eggplants, and peppers. Trees that produce bananas, oranges, lemons, and limes also grow in the valley. Relatively heavy rain falls on farmlands on the plateau. Wheat, barley, corn, potatoes, dry beans, and chickpeas grow well there. Vineyards heavy with grapes and orchards filled with apple, peach, pistachio, almond, fig, and olive trees are also found on the plateau.

Chickens are the most common livestock raised in Jordan. There are about 24 million chickens in the country. They are raised on farms and in villages. The rest of Jordan's livestock grazes on the country's sparse grassland. Herders tend to about 1.5 million sheep and 600,000 goats. These animals provide milk, cheese, and meat as well as wool to make cloth. Goatskin and sheepskin become beautiful leather goods.

A shepherd tends his flock in the highlands of Jordan.

Arabian Horses and Camels

Two kinds of livestock raised mainly in desert countries in the Middle East are Arabian horses and camels. These animals remain an important part of Jordan's Bedouin culture. The Bedouin breed many of the country's 4,000 Arabian horses. The Royal Stables in Amman have about 135 purebred Arabian horses. At one time, the Arabian horse was used in battle. It was known for its speed and endurance. Today, that speed makes them great racehorses. At full gallop, they can cover 12 feet (3.6 m) in one stride. They are also prizewinning show horses. Members of the royal family have ridden Arabian horses in events in the Olympic Games.

At one time, camels were important desert work animals. The camel's most noted characteristic is endurance. Camels can carry up to 1,100 pounds (500 kilograms) of goods for seventy days, traveling about 25 miles (45 km) a day. They can move at a steady speed of 3 miles (5 km) per hour for up to fifteen hours. Today, Jordan has about 18,000 camels. Bedouins in Wadi Rum rent their camels to tourists for rides in the desert. Members of the Desert Patrol of Jordan's army also ride camels as they check the border areas for smugglers and people entering the country illegally.

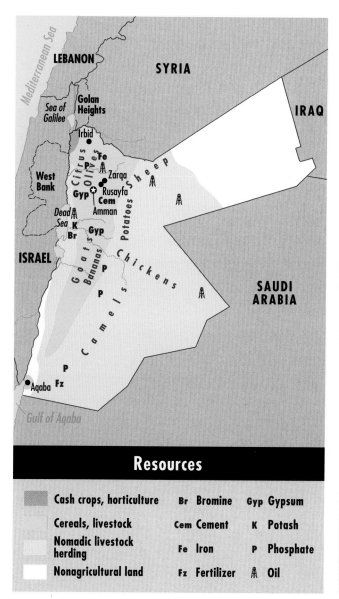

Resources

	Cash crops, horticulture	Br	Bromine	Gyp	Gypsum
	Cereals, livestock	Cem	Cement	K	Potash
	Nomadic livestock herding	Fe	Iron	P	Phosphate
	Nonagricultural land	Fz	Fertilizer	⚒	Oil

Mountains of salt pile up at the Dead Sea Salt Works, where salt is removed from the sea's water.

Mining and Manufacturing

Jordan's major minerals are phosphate rock, potash, and salt. Jordan is the world's sixth-largest phosphate producer. This mineral is used to make fertilizer, one of Jordan's major manufactured goods. Most of Jordan's potash deposits are located at the Dead Sea. Potash is used to produce chemicals such as potassium chloride. Salt deposits are found at the Dead Sea as well as in the eastern and southern deserts. These salts have industrial uses and do not find their way to dinner tables.

In the 1980s, natural gas fields were discovered near Rhisheh in the northeast. Gas from this area provides energy for a power station that generates about 12 percent

Cars fill up at a gas station in Amman. Jordan produces far less oil than its Middle Eastern neighbors.

of Jordan's electricity. Other high-quality minerals found in small amounts include copper, sand for glassmaking, feldspar and clay for ceramics, and gypsum for cement.

Fertilizers, cement, and distilled fuel oils are Jordan's leading manufactured goods. Jordan has limited oil reserves and imports crude oil from neighboring oil-rich countries. The country's only oil refinery is in Zarqa, where Jordan's only steel mill is also located.

Jordanian factories produce consumer goods such as refrigerators and cooking stoves. Automobiles are assembled in Jordan from kits of materials made in South Korea and Great Britain. Other factories produce food, clothing, textiles, shoes, and cigarettes. The production of medical drugs is a rapidly growing section of Jordan's industry.

What Jordan Grows, Makes, and Mines

Agriculture (2002)

Tomatoes	359,800 metric tons
Olives	180,900 metric tons
Cucumbers	120,300 metric tons

Manufacturing (2002)

Cement	3,455,000 metric tons
Phosphate fertilizers	459,000 metric tons
Distilled fuel oils	10,200,000 barrels

Mining (2002)

Phosphate	7,179,000 metric tons
Potash	1,174,000 metric tons
Salt	347,000 metric tons

Service Industries

Service industries make up the largest part of Jordan's economy and employ the largest number of people. Jordan's main service industries are finance, technology, trade, tourism, and transportation. The finance industry includes banking and the stock exchange.

Technology is one of the fastest-growing areas of Jordan's economy, and the government has encouraged both the development and the use of technology. People working in technology have jobs such as writing computer programs. Every year, more and more Jordanians use technology. At least 170,000 personal computers are in use. About 457,000 Jordanians use the Internet. If they don't have their own computer, they access the Internet at school or at Internet cafés.

Trade with other countries is important to the life of Jordan's people. Many of Jordan's neighbors suffer from uncertain political conditions that disrupt trade. For that reason, Jordan wants to increase trade with the United States and countries in Europe and Asia. In 2000, Jordan signed a free trade agreement with the United States, which over time will eliminate tariffs (taxes) on goods traded between the two countries. Because Jordan does not produce enough food, it must import large amounts of grains, meats, and other foods. Fuel oil, machinery, and transportation equipment are also major imports. Most of Jordan's imports come from the United States, China, and Germany. Large amounts of Jordanian goods are shipped to Iraq, India, and Saudi Arabia. Chemicals, phosphates, and potash are Jordan's major exports.

Tourism is regarded as the most important part of Jordan's economy. In 2003, almost four million people from other countries visited Jordan. They spent more than $800 million. Some of these visitors came from neighboring countries and only stayed a day or two. Others traveled through Jordan on their way to the Saudi Arabian holy city of Mecca. Many foreign visitors spend several days enjoying Jordan's historic, holy, and natural attractions. The Dead Sea, Petra, Wadi Rum, Wadi Mujib, Arab forts, Crusader castles, nature reserves, and the cities of Amman, Aqaba, and Jerash receive many tourist dinars. New resorts, hotels, and restaurants continue to be built along the Dead Sea and the Gulf of Aqaba.

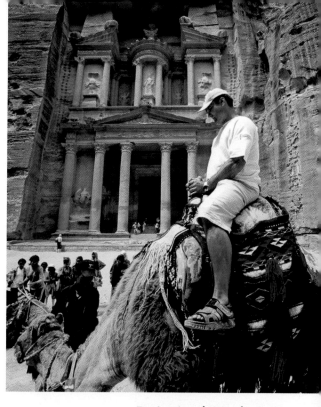

Tourism is a thriving business in Jordan. People travel from all over the world to visit Petra and other ancient sites.

Jordan's transportation system makes it possible to move people and goods easily around the country. Queen Alia International Airport is outside Amman. Aqaba has Jordan's other international airport. Royal Jordanian Airline flies to the United States, Europe, Asia, North Africa, and the Middle East. An express train links Amman with Damascus, Syria. A regular rail line also runs through Jordan from Syria to Saudi Arabia. Jordan has 4,527 miles (7,301 km) of wide, paved highways. Aqaba has Jordan's only port. From Aqaba, ferries take passengers and cars to Egypt. The port also handles about 15 million tons (14 million metric tons) of imports and exports each year.

Becoming a People

KING ABDULLAH AND THE JORDANIAN GOVERNMENT regard the people of Jordan as the country's most important resource. Every year, the government invests millions of dinars in education, health care, and welfare. With a strong, healthy, well-educated people, Jordan will become an even more secure and prosperous country. Abdullah wants his people to be united. He wants them to think of themselves as Jordanians.

Opposite: **Almost all Jordanians are Arabs.**

Students at Jordanian Yarmuk University surf the Internet.

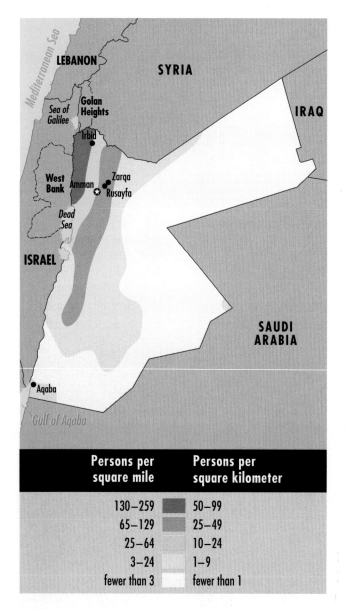

Persons per square mile		Persons per square kilometer
130–259		50–99
65–129		25–49
25–64		10–24
3–24		1–9
fewer than 3		fewer than 1

In 2005, Jordan had an estimated population of 5,759,732 people. Jordan's population is very young. About 37 percent of the people are younger than fifteen years old. Jordan averages 158 people for every square mile (61 per sq km), but the population is not spread out evenly throughout the country. About 80 percent of the people live in cities. The largest concentrations of people are in cities on the northern highland plateau. By itself, the city of Amman is home to 33 percent of Jordan's population. The farmland of the Jordan Valley also supports a large concentration of people. In addition, many people live near the wetland city of Azraq and the port city of Aqaba. Few people live in Jordan's eastern and southern deserts.

The People of Jordan

About 98 percent of Jordan's population are Arabs, which includes both Jordanians and Palestinians. They all speak the Arabic language. Most of Jordan's Arabs are Muslims, who follow the religion of Islam; a few Jordanian Arabs are Christians. Arabs have a long history in Jordan. Between 1200 B.C. and the A.D. 630s, their ancestors entered Jordan from the Arabian Peninsula to the southwest. The word *Arab* comes from a term that means "to move around," and that is what the early Arabs did. They were tribes of nomads who moved from place to place finding grazing land for their sheep and camels. About 170,000 Jordanian Arabs still live that kind of life. These people are called Bedouins. *Bedouin* comes from a term that means "people of the desert." Today's Bedouins continue to live in tents in the desert, raising sheep, camels, and horses.

Population of Jordan's Major Cities (est. 2004)

Amman	1,864,809
Zarqa	484,614
Irbid	313,121
Rusayfah	269,458
Aqaba	110,215

Many Bedouins are nomads, but they are not constantly on the move. Instead, they may camp in one place for months at a time while their animals graze on the local grasses.

Who Lives in Jordan?

Jordanian Arabs	38 %
Palestinian Arabs	60 %
Circassians and Chechens	1 %
Armenians	1 %

Palestinian Arabs make up more than half of Jordan's population. The Palestinians first arrived in large numbers in the late 1940s when the country of Israel was created after Britain left Palestine. In 1967, more Palestinians fled to Jordan when Israel gained control of the West Bank. Many Palestinians who had been working in Kuwait moved to Jordan in 1990, after Iraq seized Kuwait. Most Palestinians live in Amman, Zarqa, and other cities. The Palestinians are well educated and own many of Jordan's businesses. A large number of Palestinians are citizens of Jordan and consider it their home. About 280,000 Palestinians continue to live in thirteen refugee camps in Jordan, however. They hope someday to return to the West Bank or other areas now controlled by Israel.

A Palestinian merchant sells sheepskins in Amman.

The Armenians, Circassians, and Chechens are small, non-Arab minority groups in Jordan. Together, they make up 2 percent of the population. The Armenians are Christians, and many of them continue to speak the Armenian language. They are descended from people who fled to Syria to escape persecution by the Ottoman Turks. Later, some Armenians left Syria and settled in Jordan's northern cities.

The Circassians and Chechens were Muslims who fled religious persecution in southern Russia in the 1850s. The Ottoman Empire resettled some of them in Jordan. The Circassians built up Amman and founded Zarqa. Today, Circassians are best known as members of the king's palace honor guard. They also hold government and other army positions and own many businesses. The Chechens mainly live in Jordan's northern cities. Both the Chechens and the Circassians have their own languages.

A Circassian dance group performs at the Royal Cultural Center in Amman. An estimated twenty thousand to eighty thousand Circassians live in Jordan.

Jordanian Arabs have become a minority in their own country. To prevent violence from breaking out among Jordan's various groups, King Abdullah is working to have all the country's people think of themselves as Jordanians. Intermarriage between Jordanian and Palestinian Muslim Arabs, between Muslim Arabs and Muslim Circassians, and between Jordanian Christian Arabs and Armenian Christians is helping the king's efforts.

Jordan's Languages

Arabic is Jordan's official language. All Jordanians have this spoken language in common. Jordan's Bedouins speak the purest form of Arabic. Their language is still much like the language spoken by the Arabs who swept into the region in the 630s. This form of Arabic is called classical Arabic. It is the language in which the Qur'an was written. Modern Standard Arabic is the form used in Jordan's schools, on television, and in books and newspapers. In the Middle East and North Africa, a variety of dialects of Arabic are spoken. Within Jordan, this is true in different areas, cities, and even neighborhoods.

Although Arabic is Jordan's official language, other languages are also spoken. Armenians, Circassians, and Chechens speak their own languages at home and among friends. English has become

Common Arabic Words and Phrases

'afwan	You're welcome
aysh ismak?	What's your name?
gadaysh se'aa?	What time is it?
gadaysh hada?	How much is it?
leh	No
keefak?	How are you?
ma assalaameh	Good-bye
marhaba	Hi
min fadlak	Please
naam	Yes
shukran	Thank you

Jordan's second language. Jordanians begin learning English in elementary school. Even Bedouins are beginning to speak some English. It helps them to better serve the many English-speaking tourists who want to rent camels or to spend a night in a Bedouin camp.

Jordan has a strong school system. All children are required to attend school through tenth grade.

Body Language in Jordan

Throughout the Middle East, people often use hand gestures and head motions in place of speech. Here are some examples of Jordanian body language:

Raising the eyebrows and lifting the head up and back means "No."

Nodding downward to one side means "Yes."

Shaking the head from side to side means "I don't understand."

Placing the right hand over the heart means "No thanks."

Rubbing the palms together means "I'm finished with you (or the matter)."

Written Arabic

Although spoken Arabic has many dialects, the language is written in only one way. Written Arabic has a twenty-eight-letter alphabet. The letters have curves, loops, and horizontal lines. Some letters also have dots and geometric shapes. Each letter has more than one shape, depending on where it is placed in a word—at the beginning, in the middle, or at the end—or if the letter stands alone. There are no capital letters in Arabic. Arabic is written from right to left and from top to bottom on a page. Because of that, books, magazines, and newspapers written in Arabic open from the left.

With its flowing, curving letters, written Arabic can be quite beautiful. Sometimes Arabic is written in calligraphy. This elaborate writing style is often used in Arabic artwork or in special books, such as the Qur'an. Some archaeologists have found markings similar to the Arabic alphabet carved into stone in Petra. They think that those marks might be early examples of written Arabic.

The Arabic Alphabet

a	ا	d*	ض
b	ب	t*	ط
t	ت	z*	ظ
th	ث	a pause	ع
g	ج	gh	غ
h	ح	f	ف
kh	خ	q	ق
d	د	k	ك
dh	ذ	l	ل
r	ر	m	م
z	ز	n	ن
s	س	h	ه
sh	ش	w	و
s*	ص	y	ي

*Harder sounds

Education

Jordan has one of the Middle East's best education systems. It ranks 27th among 102 countries around the world in quality of education. Since the 1990s, Jordan's Ministry of Education has overseen an ongoing program to reform and improve Jordan's schools. Textbooks are revised and updated. Teachers

There are twenty-eight letters in the Arabic alphabet. Many of the letters include dots above or below the main shape.

Girls in a computer class in a Jordanian school

are trained in better ways to instruct students. For example, they are taught to lead class discussions and to help students develop critical-thinking skills. More schools are being built, especially in rural areas. More math, science, and technology are being added to the curriculum. All of these reforms are designed to encourage creativity and to develop job skills in Jordan's students.

Activities in Jordanian Middle Schools

Jordanian middle-school students have a full schedule of classes. They study Arabic, English, math, science, history, religion—both Islam and Christianity—computer skills, physical education, art, and music. School starts at 8 A.M. and ends at 1:30 P.M. The school year runs from the end of August to the middle of June. Jordan's public schools also offer after-school activities, such as sports, music lessons, and computer classes.

Education is free and required for all children ages six through fifteen. Attendance in public high schools is also free, but students must pay for their books. At age sixteen, many boys and girls stop attending school, usually because of the cost. At public universities and community colleges, students pay a small tuition and can apply for financial aid. The parents of children in private elementary and secondary schools and colleges pay full tuition. Currently, Jordan has several community colleges, eight public universities, and twelve private universities. At the university level, about half of the students today are women.

Students listen to a lecture at the University of Jordan. About half of Jordanian college students are women.

Becoming a People **91**

One Main Religion

JORDAN'S CONSTITUTION STATES THAT THE COUNTRY'S OFFICIAL religion is Islam and that the king must be a Muslim. It also states that all religions are tolerated and that Jordanians will not be discriminated against because of their religion. Nevertheless, because 96 percent of the population is Muslim, Islam influences all areas of life in Jordan—even for non-Muslims. For example, Muslims believe that pigs are an unclean animal. Therefore, pigs are not raised in Jordan and pork is not eaten. Jordan's official weekend begins on Thursday evening as Muslims prepare for their Sabbath on Friday.

Opposite: **A girl reads from the Qur'an at a mosque in Amman.**

Grooms and their brides, hidden completely behind veils, attend a mass wedding in Amman.

Religions of Jordan

Sunni Muslim	95%
Christian	4%
Other Muslims: Shi'i, Druze	1%

The Teachings of Islam

The Arab prophet Muhammad (570–632) founded Islam in 610 in Mecca in what is now Saudi Arabia. *Islam* means "submission to God's will." Muhammad was instructed through visions from Allah (God) to preach about Allah's power and goodness. Muhammad's followers later wrote down these visions in the Qur'an, the Muslim holy book. Allah is the same God that the Christians and Jews worship. Muhammad accepted the Old Testament of the Jews and the New Testament of the Christians. However, Muhammad did not accept Jesus as the son of God. Instead, Muslims consider Jesus one of the prophets, and Muhammad the last and final prophet. Muhammad believed that he was to spread Islam throughout the world. In the 630s, Muhammad's followers brought Islam with them when they swept through what is now Jordan. At that time, Jordan was an unnamed part of Greater Syria.

The words of Allah in the Qur'an provide instruction for most areas of daily life: the importance of the family, the roles of women and children, how foods should be prepared, what foods should not be eaten, the importance of cleanliness and modesty in dress, and that living things should not be portrayed in art. Muslims believe that the Qur'an is God's last word to man.

The Five Pillars of Islam are the Qur'an's most important rules. The first pillar, *shahadah*, tells Muslims that they must profess their faith by saying, "There is no God except God and Muhammad is his prophet." The second pillar, *salat,*

requires prayer five times a day—at sunrise, midmorning, mid-afternoon, sunset, and night. In villages, a person called a *muezzin* calls Muslims to prayer from the mosque's minaret, or tower. In the cities, the call is broadcast with tapes over loudspeakers. These daily prayers can take place in a mosque, at home, or outdoors. During prayer, Muslims kneel and bow down facing Mecca—the location of the sacred shrine of the Ka'ba (the Black Stone), around which the pilgrims walk.

Five times a day Muslims stop what they are doing and pray facing Mecca.

Each year, millions of Muslims make a pilgrimage to Mecca. While in Mecca, all male pilgrims wear a simple white garment called an *ihram* to show that they are all equal in the eyes of Allah.

The third pillar, *zakat*, requires that Muslims give gifts of charity to the poor. *Sawm*, which means "fasting," is the fourth pillar. Fasting takes place during the entire month of Ramadan, the ninth month in the Islamic year. During each day of Ramadan, Muslims eat and drink nothing from sunrise to sunset. After dark, they have a large meal with their families. During Ramadan, most restaurants in Jordan are only open in the evening. Other businesses stay open fewer hours during the day. The last pillar is the *hajj*, the pilgrimage to Mecca. If financially and physically possible, all Muslims are expected to make this trip once in their lives. The hajj takes place two months after Ramadan.

Friday is the Islamic Sabbath. About noon on Fridays, Jordan's Muslims gather for prayer in their mosques. Women and men pray separately. Someone reads from the Qur'an, and an *imam*, a preacher or spiritual adviser, gives a sermon.

A man at a mosque reads from the Qur'an. Most mosques have different sections for men and women.

Sects of Islam in Jordan

After Muhammad's death, his followers disagreed on who should be the new leader, called the *caliph*. Islam split into two branches, Sunni and Shi'i. Today, most Jordanians are Sunni Muslims. The Shi'i are a tiny minority in Jordan. Most Shi'i in Jordan are the descendants of Chechens, who fled from Russia to Jordan in the late 1800s.

The other main Muslim sect in Jordan is the Druze. This sect is an offshoot of the Shi'i. The Druze don't follow all the rules of Islam. They do not fast during Ramadan. They don't pray in mosques. Thursday is their Sabbath. In addition, they regard one of their founders as divine. The Druze also believe in reincarnation, the idea that after death, a person's soul is reborn into a new body. Jordan's Druze originally came from Syria. Today, the Druze live mainly in northern Jordan, close to the Syrian border and near the city of Zarqa.

Muslims in Amman gather for Friday prayers. More men than women go to mosques to pray.

Sufism

Sufism is not another sect of Islam. Instead, it is the mystical dimension of both Sunni and Shi'i Islam. Sufis try to detach themselves from the world and its distractions. They do this through prayer and fasting. In groups, Sufis chant, jump, and sway back and forth until they lose touch with the material world and feel God in every part of their body. Other Sufis become whirling dervishes. They believe that by spinning in a circle until they cannot feel anything, they become united with God. In Jordan, the dance of the whirling dervishes has become a form of entertainment. Groups of dervishes perform in hotels in Amman.

Muslim Holidays

The Islamic calendar has 354 days rather than 365 like the Western calendar. As a result, Muslim holidays fall on different dates in the Western calendar each year. Muharram is the first month in the Islamic calendar. New Year's celebrations, which are marked by feasting, can go on for ten days.

One of the main Islamic feasts is Eid al-Fitr, which means "the breaking of the fast." This great feast comes at the end of Ramadan—the month of fasting—and lasts for three days. Jordanians celebrate this feast with special foods, such as sticky desserts filled with fruits and nuts. Many Jordanians also buy new clothes at this time. Then they visit family and friends.

Jordan's Famous Mosques

Every Jordanian village and town has a mosque. Each mosque is positioned so that during prayer, the faithful are facing Mecca. Jordan's largest mosques, the King Abdullah Mosque and the Abu Darwish Mosque, are in Amman. In 1989, King Hussein had the King Abdullah Mosque built in honor of his grandfather. Its blue dome makes the mosque stand out as an Amman landmark. A huge three-ringed chandelier hangs under the dome. About seven thousand Muslims can worship in the prayer hall. The outdoor courtyard holds another three thousand worshippers. The Abu Darwish Mosque, which was completed in 1961, was built by Amman's Circassian community. Its unusual black-and-white-checked stone design stands out among Amman's mainly white stone buildings.

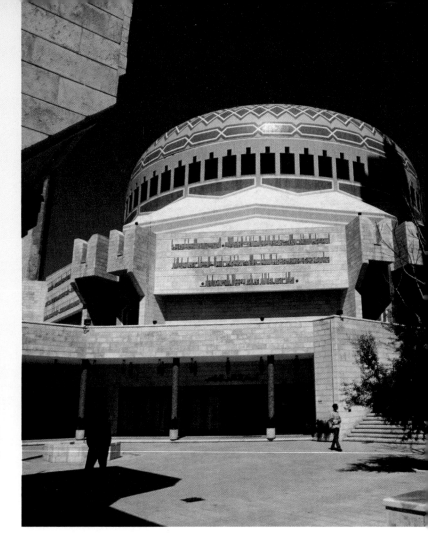

Eid al-Adha, the feast of the sacrifice, marks the end of the hajj, the pilgrimage to Mecca. This feast also lasts three days. Eid al-Adha recalls Abraham's willingness to sacrifice his son as God had commanded. Seeing Abraham's obedience, God had Abraham kill a lamb instead of his son. Today, for Eid al-Adha, Muslims have a cow, goat, or lamb slaughtered. Then they give one-third of it to the poor and another third to relatives. They prepare the last third for the family feast.

Christians in Jordan

Before the Arabs brought Islam to Jordan, most of the people who lived there were Christian. Jesus, the founder of Christianity, was born in Bethlehem and died in Jerusalem. At that time, both cities were in Roman-controlled Palestine. Today, they are in the Israeli-controlled West Bank. Christians believe that during his life, Jesus crossed the Jordan River into what is now Bethany-Beyond-the-Jordan, where he was baptized in the river. In A.D. 70, the Roman Empire pressured Jerusalem's Christians and Jews to give up their religions. As a result, many Christians fled and settled in Jordan.

Jesus is said to have been baptized in Bethany-Beyond-the-Jordan. Today, the channels that once carried the baptismal water have been restored.

Today, about 4 percent of Jordanians are Christian. Most of them are Arabs. Most Jordanian Christians belong to the Greek Orthodox Church. Other Jordanian Christians belong to the Armenian Orthodox Church and to the Greek, Armenian, and Roman Catholic churches. A small number of Jordanians belong to Protestant churches, such as the Anglican and Evangelical Lutheran churches. Karak, Madaba, Salt, Ajlun, and Amman have large Christian populations.

Jordan has many famous churches. One of the best known is the Greek Orthodox Church of St. George in Madaba.

The largest number of Jordanian Christians belong to the Greek Orthodox Church.

In the late 1800s, this church was built over an older Byzantine church. During construction in 1884, a mosaic was found on the old church's floor. The mosaic was a map of the Jewish and Christian holy sites in the Middle East. Dating to A.D. 560, it is the oldest existing map of the Middle East.

The major Christian holidays are Christmas and Easter. Jordan's Orthodox communities use a different calendar, so they celebrate these holidays on different days from its Catholic and Protestant communities. In modern Amman, Christmas is celebrated in much the same way as in the United States. Stores are decorated with Christmas trees, children have their picture taken with Santa Claus, and choirs sing carols in public places. In Jordan's villages, Christmas is celebrated in a more spiritual manner. There are no Christmas trees or stockings. On Christmas Day, Christian families attend Mass. Some also visit the graves of family members. Later in the day, families and friends visit one another and share meals. Children receive gifts, usually new clothes, from their parents.

A Greek Orthodox priest releases a dove during a celebration on Epiphany. Epiphany commemorates the day that the three wise men are supposed to have arrived with gifts for the baby Jesus.

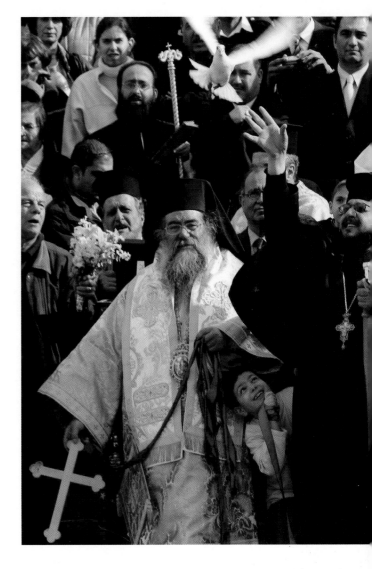

CHAPTER NINE

Traditional Arts in New Settings

JORDAN HAS A RICH CULTURAL HERITAGE. ITS TRADITIONAL culture ranges from embroidery, weaving, and glassblowing to Bedouin storytelling. Jordan also has a long history of music, art, and architecture. More recently, Jordanian writers have made vital contributions to world literature. Sports, too, are an important part of modern life.

Opposite: **Paintings dating back to the 700s can still be seen on the ceiling of Qasr Amra, a desert castle in eastern Jordan.**

A man plays a *rababah*, a traditional Arab instrument with just one string.

Traditional Crafts

For hundreds of years, Jordanians—especially Bedouins—have worked with cloth, glass, and clay to make beautiful objects for everyday use. As Bedouins and villagers began moving to Jordan's cities, some of these crafts started to die out. In the 1980s, Jordan's government and private groups began programs to reverse that trend. Now, several hundred men and women make their living keeping alive Jordan's traditional crafts and designs. The designs on the crafts are usually geometric patterns, flowers, fruits, and calligraphy. Islamic rules forbid portraying people or animals in artwork. Many of the crafts are sold to tourists.

Each tribe and village has its own design that is used in embroidered and woven goods. The flower, feather, and geometric patterns and designs in Jordanian embroidered fabrics are especially beautiful. Jordanian women use embroidery threads of red, purple, gold, pink, orange, and green. The bright colors stand out on traditional black or white dresses. Cushions and pillows also have intricately embroidered designs. Both men and women weave cloth from sheep's wool and goat and camel hair. The woven cloth is made into small prayer rugs, large carpets, and fabric for tents and cushions.

Pottery and glassblowing are traditional Jordanian crafts that had been dying out but were revived after the 1967 war with Israel. Many Palestinian potters and glassblowers emigrated from the West Bank to Jordan and set up shops in Amman. These crafters make items such as decorative ceramic tiles, hand-painted jugs and bowls, glasses, vases, and

oil lamps. The glassblowers also make *nargiles*, large water pipes that Jordanian men use to smoke tobacco.

Another Jordanian craft is making sand bottles. In Petra and Aqaba, people make designs with various colors of sand in clear glass bottles. Popular designs include camels, palm trees, and swirls of color. The colored sand comes from the many varieties of Jordan's sandstone.

A glassblower works with a melted ball of glass. Observing glassblowers in their workshops has become popular among tourists in Jordan.

Traditional Arts in New Settings **107**

Legend has it that the oud was invented by a grandson of Adam, supposedly the first man on Earth. In fact, ouds date back at least five thousand years.

Music and Dance

Arab music sounds quite different from Western music. Sometimes, there is more than one rhythm or beat in a song. Many musical instruments played in Jordan produce sounds that are unlike those of Western instruments. The *oud*, a lute-like instrument, has one bass string and five or six pairs of double strings. The one-stringed *rababah* makes a wailing sound. The *mizmarmunjwiz*, the *nay*, and the *gasaba* are types of flutes. The *gerbeh*, or bagpipes, are usually played by military groups in parades. A small flat drum called a *tabla* rests on a player's lap. The *durbakkah* is a large earthenware drum that stands on the floor. Most of the time, traditional instruments accompany singers. Sometimes, they are used in bands and orchestras with modern musical instruments.

For the most part, people in the Middle East, including Jordanians, don't identify singers and musicians as being from one Middle Eastern country or another. Instead, they are just thought of as Arab. One musician who is identified with Jordan is Omar Abdallah. He is known for his patriotic songs, such as "Hashemi, Hashemi," which honors the Hashemite kingdom. On the other end of the musical spectrum is Zade Dirani. He is a young composer and pianist who blends Arabic music with Western new-age sounds. After Muslim terrorists attacked the United States in 2001, Dirani made a concert tour across the United States. He played in living rooms, churches, schools, and hospitals as a way to educate Americans about Arab culture.

Jordanians have many opportunities to listen to music. Cassettes and CDs of Jordanian and Western music are readily available. Small bands play in cafés throughout Jordan. The National Jordanian Orchestra gives concerts at the Performing Arts Center in Amman.

Several dances unique to the Middle East are part of Jordan's culture. The *debkah* is mainly performed at weddings or other celebrations with large groups of people. In this dance with much stomping of feet, men or women hold hands to form a circle and then move to the music. Men and women do not dance together. The *sahjeh* is a Bedouin dance in which men act out stories of past heroes. The Circassian sword dance is fast paced and exciting. Many young Jordanians dance to more modern beats in Amman's nightclubs.

Bedouins perform a dance in Amman. Many Bedouins wear traditional headdresses.

Literature

Until the 1900s, most of Jordan's literature was not written down. Instead, Bedouins passed on their myths, other stories, and history through storytelling. Recently, university teachers and students began writing these stories down. Otherwise, the stories would be lost as younger Bedouins move to cities. Jordan's writers today use some of the same themes as early storytellers. They include love, war, and honor. Many stories and poems are also about changes occurring in society and the role of women. Some of Jordan's well-known writers come from a Palestinian background. The Palestinians have a long tradition of written literature. Because of this, Palestinian Jordanians are sometimes credited with developing Jordan's written literature.

Jordan's best-known poet, however, was not Palestinian. The poems of Mustafa Wahbi al-Tal (1899–1949) examined the important issues of his time, such as Arab nationalism. The novels of Abd al-Rahman Munif are popular in Jordan. Born in Amman in 1933 to a Saudi father and a Jordanian mother, he was awarded the Sultan al-Uways Award, the highest honor for Arabic writing. Fadia Faqir was born in Amman in 1956. Her novel *Pillars of Salt* is set in the cities and countryside of Jordan in the 1920s and 1930s. It deals with the rights of women and traditional Bedouin values. Ibrahim Nasrallah, one of the best-known Palestinian-Jordanian writers, was born in a refugee camp in Amman in 1954. He has written many novels and poems.

Abd al-Rahman Munif was one of the Arab world's greatest writers. Many of his novels deal with the influence of oil companies in a corrupt Middle Eastern country.

The Nabateans carved tombs and temples into the soft rock at Petra two thousand years ago.

Art and Architecture

Jordan's architectural treasures have been preserved in its ancient cities. One of the oldest and most amazing is the rose-red city of Petra. More than two thousand years ago, Nabatean Arabs began carving an entire city from the side of a mountain. They decorated the buildings with carved heads of gods and goddesses, horses, flowers, and mythical monsters. Over the years, they built temples, a church, tombs, and homes. An amphitheater that seated three thousand was also partially carved into the rock. Archaeologists believe that about thiry thousand people lived in Petra.

Amman and Jerash have some of the world's best-preserved Roman ruins. The ruins at Jerash include arches as tall as 43

Sixty-five pillars encircle the oval plaza at Jerash. They were constructed in the first century A.D.

feet (13 m). A stadium there has stables and a track where chariot races are reenacted. The Citadel area of Amman has a huge Roman amphitheater, a smaller amphitheater for musical performances, and a complex of what were once fountains and a swimming pool. Remains of the Umayyad Palace from about A.D. 720 are also part of the Citadel. Today, Amman is known as the "white city." Most of its newer buildings are made from white limestone. Some homes are built so that more levels can be added to them. In this way, homes on top of homes can be built for sons who marry and need a place to live with their wife.

Qasr Amra is Jordan's best-preserved desert castle. Built during the Umayyad dynasty as a retreat and hunting lodge,

Jerash Festival of Culture and Arts

The first Jerash Festival took place in 1981. Since then, this international festival has been held every summer. The Roman amphitheaters and the Temple of Artemis serve as stages for singers, orchestras, and plays. Many of the performers are Jordanians, including Circassian folklore groups, the Jordanian Children's Theatre, and the Young Musicians of Jordan. Groups from other Middle Eastern countries are well represented. In addition, a ballet group from Russia, dance and music groups from the United States, and musicians from the Czech Republic, Sudan, Pakistan, Sweden, Austria, and Lithuania have added to the international flavor.

this castle is famous for the colorful paintings on the walls of its baths. Human and animal forms are part of the frescoes. They were either painted before the ban on human and animal forms in Islamic art, or the artists decided to ignore the ruling because they were working in a desert outpost. Qasr Amra includes some of the oldest baths built by Arabs.

Southwest of Madaba are the ruins of the town of Umm-al-Rasas. This town has ruins of sixteen Byzantine churches. Many of their mosaic floors have been well preserved. The town is also said to be the place where Muhammad first learned about the need to worship one God.

Art in the form of paintings and sculptures is fairly new in Jordan. Fahrelnissa Zeid (1901–1991) was one of Jordan's earliest artists. During the 1920s and 1930s, exhibits of her large oil portraits and pen-and-ink drawings were held in Europe and the United States. Zeid taught art to other Jordanian women, some of whom also became artists. One of them, Suha Shoman, has done many abstract paintings of Petra. Today, Mona Saudi is Jordan's best-known artist. Her abstract stone sculptures are filled with emotion.

Another well-known Jordanian artist, Omar Bsoul, paints scenes of traditional life in Jordan. Figures in the paintings of Ahmad Nawash float around the canvas in dark and disturbing ways. Another of Jordan's famous artists is the political cartoonist Emad Hajjaj. His best-known character is Abu Mahjoob, which means "father of the hidden." Through this character, Hajjaj conveys the message that much is revealed by trying to hide things. Hajjaj's cartoons have appeared in many Jordanian newspapers.

Art galleries and museums are new to Jordan. Jordan's first art museum, the National Gallery of Fine Arts, opened in 1980 in Amman. This museum has exhibits of contemporary Jordanian paintings, sculptures, and pottery. In 1992, Dar al-Funun, which means "house of arts," opened in Amman. This complex includes a small art gallery, an art library, and a workshop for Jordanian and visiting painters and sculptors.

Athlete of the Year

Every year, Jordanians vote for the year's best athlete. In the 2004 competition, Yasmine Khair, a young gymnast, was the winner. Khair was born in 1987 in Amman. In 2004, she won two gold and four silver medals in the Pan Arab Games. She hopes to qualify for the Olympic Games in 2008.

Fadi Abu Latifa (in red) of the Jordanian national team fights for the ball during a match against Saudi Arabia.

Sports

The most popular sport in Jordan is soccer. Children and young men play this game at school, on playgrounds, and in parks. Several professional teams compete in a league. The best players from those teams make up the national soccer team. That team competes in international games, such as the qualifying games for the World Cup. In recent years, Jordan's national soccer team placed first in the 1997 and 1999 Pan Arab Games.

Many Jordanians enjoy playing other sports. Families in Amman make use of the sports complex there to swim or to play tennis, squash, or basketball. Swimming, snorkeling, scuba diving, and waterskiing are favorite activities in the Gulf of Aqaba. Wadi Rum and the Dana Nature Reserve provide hiking trails and hills for climbing. Each year in April, runners can take part in the Dead Sea Ultra Marathon of 31 miles (50 km). This race, which starts in Amman and ends at the Dead Sea, is about 5 miles (7 km) longer than a regular marathon.

Family, Food, and Fun

LIKE MOST PEOPLE AROUND THE WORLD, JORDANIANS enjoy socializing with family and friends. Feasts of delicious foods are usually the highlight of these gatherings. Jordanians, like other Arab people, are well-known for their generosity and hospitality. Such kindness can be traced back to the Bedouin tradition of welcoming desert travelers in need of food, water, and shelter. Today, shopkeepers offer customers tea or coffee. Visitors from other countries should not be surprised if a Jordanian invites them home for lunch or dinner.

Opposite: **A Jordanian family enjoys a day in the country.**

One of the most popular drinks in Jordan is mint tea with lots of sugar.

Family Life

Family is the center of Jordanian life. Being married and having children are regarded as duties. Jordanians often feel sorry for unmarried people or couples without children. Children are thought of as blessings. When the first male child is born, the father and mother become known by his name. For example, if the child's name is Muhammad, the father becomes Abu ("father of") Muhammad, and the mother becomes Umm ("mother of") Muhammad. These new names are used by family and close friends.

Jordanian Weddings

A wedding is the most expensive event in a Jordanian's life, and the celebration goes on for several days. The actual wedding ceremony is the signing of the marriage contract in front of witnesses. Then the groom and his male relatives and friends celebrate outside the bride's house while the women celebrate inside. Rather than getting married in traditional clothing, most brides today prefer a white wedding gown and their grooms prefer a black suit. Because weddings are so expensive, group wedding ceremonies have become more common.

Some married women in Jordan's cities work outside the home, but most do not. Within most families, the husband works and the wife stays home to cook, take care of the house, and raise the children.

Within the more traditional Muslim homes, men and women have separate rooms. Men entertain their friends in the front room of the home. Women talk and eat with their friends in another room. The only men with whom women interact socially are relatives. If a woman has contact with a man who isn't a relative, she has dishonored the family. Sometimes, the woman's father or brothers avenge the dishonor by killing her. For centuries, these "honor crimes" have gone unpunished. Currently, about twenty-five Jordanian women a year are killed for this reason. King Abdullah, Queen Rania, and some legislators have tried unsuccessfully to pass laws prohibiting these crimes. At the most, men who have committed "honor crimes" are held in jail for a few months.

A Taste of Jordan

Food plays an important part in everyday Jordanian life. Favorite family recipes are passed on from mother to daughter. Among the Bedouin, different clans or tribes have their own secret recipes for traditional dishes.

Most Jordanians eat three meals each day. Breakfast usually consists of *khubz* (a flat, round bread), cheese, cold cuts, and olives. Pieces of the bread are dipped into *labaneh*, strained yogurt that is like a soft cream cheese, or into *zaater*, which is olive oil and oregano. Khubz is also spread with butter and jam. The main meal of the day is served between 2 P.M. and 4 P.M. By that time, children are home from school. Workers take a lunch break and join their families for this meal. It generally includes rice and a stew of meat and vegetables, such as *maloukhieh* (spinach, chicken pieces, hot green pepper, and lemon). Khubz is also served and might be used to scoop up the rice and stew. In the evening at 8 P.M. or later, Jordanians have dinner, which includes the same kinds of foods that were served at breakfast. If Jordanians are entertaining friends or family, then the usual midday foods would be served for dinner instead.

Bedouin women enjoy a meal while sitting on a rock. Usually, Bedouin men and women eat separately.

Mensaf: Jordan's National Dish

The national dish of Jordan is *mensaf*. It is served on special occasions, such as birthdays, weddings, and religious holidays. Mensaf is made of large chunks of lamb cooked in a yogurt sauce and served on a bed of rice that is sprinkled with roasted pine nuts. Mensaf is served on a huge tray—about 30 inches (80 cm) in diameter. Sometimes, the lamb's head is placed in the center of the tray. The tongue and eyeballs are saved as special treats for the honored guest. Mensaf is usually eaten standing up; if the meal is served on the floor, it is eaten sitting down. Diners scoop up small fistfuls of mensaf and toss it into their mouths so their fingers do not touch their lips. In a home or restaurant in a city, diners might use a fork.

Shoppers in markets are often drawn to the sweet smell of baklava.

Sometimes, the main meal or dinner might include appetizers, called *mezze*. Examples of mezze include dips, stuffed grape leaves, and salads. *Hummus* (a paste of cooked, ground chickpeas, ground sesame seeds, garlic, and lemon) and baba *ghanoush* (mashed eggplant and ground sesame seeds) are popular dips. Grape leaves are stuffed with meat and vegetables. *Tabouleh* is a salad made with tomatoes, parsley, cracked wheat, sesame seeds, garlic, and lemon juice. *Fattoush* is another popular salad.

All meals are followed by coffee or tea. The coffee is strong. It is boiled three times and flavored with cardamom. Guests indicate that they've had enough coffee by tipping their empty cup from side to side. Tea in Jordan is very sweet. It is often flavored with crushed mint and lots of sugar.

Jordanians satisfy their sweet tooth with a variety of rich desserts. *Knafeh*, a special dessert, is made with layers of shredded dough and soft cheese that is drizzled with a syrupy rose-water sauce and topped with pistachios. Another sweet, sticky dessert is *baklava*. It is made with layers of phyllo dough, crushed pistachios or almonds, and orange or rose-water syrup. In the summer, watermelon served with salty white cheese and honeydew melons are refreshing sweets.

Jordanians sometimes grab quick snacks or light meals at fast-food restaurants or food stands. A few McDonald's, Burger

Making a Jordanian Salad

Fattoush is an easy-to-make salad that is popular in Jordan and in other countries of the Middle East.

Salad:
2 cups chopped lettuce
2 chopped tomatoes
1 peeled and chopped cucumber
1 tablespoon dried mint
¼ cup chopped parsley
1½ cups toasted and crumbled pita bread
(or other toasted bread crumbs or croutons)

Salad dressing:
¼ cup lemon juice
¼ cup olive oil
½ teaspoon salt
Pinch of black pepper

To make fattoush, first toss all the salad ingredients together in a bowl. Place all the dressing ingredients together in a jar with a tight lid and shake until blended. Pour the salad dressing over the salad. Divide the salad into three or four portions, place on salad plates, and enjoy!

For a quick snack, many Jordanians buy a shwarma filled with meat and vegetables.

Kings, and Pizza Huts have popped up in Jordan's largest cities. But most Jordanians still enjoy their own traditional fast-food sandwiches. *Shwarma* is slices of chicken or lamb cut from a revolving vertical spit. The meat is mixed with onions and tomatoes and stuffed into a piece of khubz. *Falafel* is khubz filled with deep-fried balls of spicy chickpea paste, pickled vegetables, tomatoes, and yogurt.

From Tents to Flats and Villas

Bedouin encampments of black goat-hair tents can still be found in Jordan's vast desert. These long tents are held up by tall wooden poles. The Bedouin can easily set up and take down their tents as they move in search of water and grazing land for their animals. Brightly colored carpets cover the ground in each tent. During the day, blankets and pillows are stacked along the sides of the tents. The tents' sides or flaps are kept closed to keep cold air and blowing sand out. On mild days, the flaps are opened to let a breeze circulate through the tent. Most tents are divided into two or three rooms separated by cloth walls. Men eat and sleep in one room, and women eat and sleep in another.

The Bedouins' long tents are easy to put up and to take down.

Homes in Jordan's farming villages are small. Like the Bedouins' tents, they usually have only two or three rooms, and the furnishings are similar. Most of Jordan's villagers have running water, but many do not have electricity.

In Jordan's cities, most people live in apartments or condominiums, which they call flats. A typical family's flat has a kitchen, living room, dining room, two bedrooms, a bathroom, and a guest room. Jordanian kitchens have cabinets, counters, a sink, a refrigerator, and a range. Their bathrooms have a toilet, sink, and shower. Because water is scarce in Jordan, it is delivered twice a week in some areas and stored in tanks on rooftops. From there, water travels through a plumbing system to reach individual flats. As in the United States, families usually eat their meals in the kitchen and use the dining room for meals with guests. Large decorative rugs cover the floors, and elaborate chandeliers hang from the ceilings. Furniture—such as tables, chairs, couches, and bedroom sets—is similar in style to what is found in American or European homes.

Jordanians who live in cities or suburbs might own a house, which is called a villa. An average two-story villa has four bedrooms, three bathrooms, a living room, a dining room, a kitchen, and a guest room. Villas have small yards with flowers, shrubs, and trees that grow well with little water.

A Jordanian family relaxes in their living room. Some families use rugs to brighten the walls as well as to warm the floor.

Traditional and Modern Clothing

Traditional Bedouin clothing was originally designed to make life in the desert more comfortable. Long, loose-fitting robes and gowns kept men and women cooler during hot summer days. Layers of these clothes warmed them during winters or through cool summer nights. Thick-soled sandals enabled the Bedouin to walk easily on the hot, shifting desert sands. Headdresses protected them from the heat and from blowing sand. Today, Jordan's Bedouins wear pieces of their traditional clothing, but most mix this with Western clothing.

Many Jordanian women cover their hair with a hijab. But many of those same women also wear Western clothing.

Some Jordanian Muslim women wear the traditional scarf called the *hijab*, which covers the woman's head, hair, and shoulders. A hijab can be pulled across the nose and mouth, either for modesty or to keep the sand out. Bedouin women also wear heavily embroidered, long, black dresses. The embroidery pattern indicates the woman's village or clan. These dresses are worn every day in the desert. In Jordan's cities, women wear these dresses for special occasions.

Some Arab men wear headcloths called *keyfiyahs*. In summer, the men wear white keyfiyahs. In cooler weather, they wear heavier red and white or black and white keyfiyahs. The keyfiyah is held in place by a black cord called an *agal*. Keyfiyahs are worn with ankle-length gowns called *jalabiyyehs* or with Western-style suits. Some men also wear loose-fitting trousers under their jalabiyyehs.

Leisure Activities and Holidays

Men enjoy coffee, tea, and conversation at a coffee-house in Amman.

Some traditional activities continue to be popular with Jordanians. Some Jordanian girls still play *hajli*, a kind of hopscotch. Many girls also play with dolls. A favorite doll is Fulla, who is similar to the American Barbie doll. Fulla is packaged in a pink box with a pink prayer rug. She is dressed modestly in a white hijab and long coat or in a black hijab and long, black dress. Some boys play *ghalool*, a game of marbles. Men spend evenings in coffeehouses. There they drink coffee, talk, play *tric-trac* (backgammon) and *shutterunge* (a game played on a chessboard), and smoke the nargile. Women sometimes get together at a restaurant for lunch or meet to go shopping in covered markets called *souqs*.

Many Jordanian families do not have enough money for vacations. Instead, they take short trips. They might go on a picnic or spend a day at the Dead Sea or on the beach at Aqaba. They might also go camping in Wadi Rum or the Dana Nature Reserve. Families with more money take longer vacations to Lebanon, Egypt, Dubai, Turkey, or Cyprus. These families might also stay overnight at a hotel at the Dead Sea, Petra, or Aqaba. To encourage more Jordanians to travel within the country, King Abdullah II created the two-day weekend. Government offices, schools, and some businesses are now closed on Saturdays as well on Fridays, the Muslim Sabbath.

Besides the two-day weekend, Jordanians also get a break from work and school on national holidays. Independence Day, Arab Revolt Day, and important anniversaries like the king's enthronement are the main nonreligious holidays. In Amman, these events are marked by military parades of soldiers and marching bands. Speeches by the king and performances by various youth groups take place in Amman's sports stadium. King Abdullah takes pride in the Jordanian people, and they take pride in their country and its history.

National Holidays in Jordan

New Year's Day	January 1
King Abdullah II's Birthday	January 30
Labor Day	May 1
Independence Day	May 25
King Abdullah II Enthronement Day	June 9
Arab Revolt and Army Day	June 10
King Hussein Remembrance Day	November 14

Muslim holy days are based on the Islamic calendar, which is eleven days shorter than the Western calendar. The following holy days are also public holidays, but they change dates from year to year.

Eid al-Fitr	Feast at the end of Ramadan
Eid al-Adha	Feast of Sacrifice
Moulid al-Nebi	The Birth of Muhammad

Timeline

Jordan History		World History	
People begin living in Jordan.	ca. 150,000 B.C.		
People begin living in settlements in Jordan.	ca. 17,000–8000 B.C.		
		2500 B.C.	Egyptians build the Pyramids and the Sphinx in Giza.
The kingdoms of Gilead, Ammon, Moab, and Edom develop in western Jordan.	ca. 1900–1200 B.C.		
Jordan is under the control of the Assyrian and Babylonian empires.	722–539 B.C.		
Arab Nabateans move into southern Jordan.	600s B.C.	563 B.C.	The Buddha is born in India.
Jordan becomes part of the Persian Empire.	539 B.C.		
Jordan comes under Greek rule.	332 B.C.		
The Nabatean kingdom becomes part of the Roman Empire.	A.D. 106		
Jordan becomes part of the Byzantine Empire.	324	A.D. 313	The Roman emperor Constantine recognizes Christianity.
Arab Muslims take control of Jordan.	636	610	The Prophet Muhammad begins preaching a new religion called Islam.
		1054	The Eastern (Orthodox) and Western (Roman) Catholic Churches break apart.
		1066	William the Conqueror defeats the English in the Battle of Hastings.
		1095	Pope Urban II proclaims the First Crusade.
The Crusades begin.	1098		
Saladin defeats the Crusaders.	1188	1215	King John seals the Magna Carta.
		1300s	The Renaissance begins in Italy.
		1347	The Black Death sweeps through Europe.
		1453	Ottoman Turks capture Constantinople, conquering the Byzantine Empire.
		1492	Columbus arrives in North America.
Jordan becomes part of the Ottoman Empire.	1516	1500s	The Reformation leads to the birth of Protestantism.
		1776	The Declaration of Independence is signed.

Jordan History

The Ottomans are defeated in World War I.	1918
Britain is given a mandate over Palestine, which includes Jordan.	1920
Britain recognizes Abdullah as head of the Emirate of Transjordan.	1923
Jordan gains independence from Britain.	1946
During the Arab-Israeli War, Jordan gains control of eastern Jerusalem and the West Bank.	1948
King Abdullah is assassinated.	1951
King Hussein becomes the official leader of Jordan.	1953
Jordan loses the West Bank to Israel during the Six-Day War.	1967
A civil war known as Black September breaks out between Palestinian and Jordanian forces.	1970
Jordan gives up control of the West Bank.	1988
Multiparty elections are held for the first time since 1956.	1993
Jordan and Israel sign a peace agreement.	1994
King Hussein dies; Abdullah II succeeds his father as king.	1999
Jordan signs a free-trade agreement with the United States.	2000
Construction begins on a dam on the Yarmuk River.	2004
Al Qaeda suicide bombers attack three hotels in Amman, killing sixty people.	2005

World History

1789	The French Revolution begins.
1865	The American Civil War ends.
1914	World War I breaks out.
1917	The Bolshevik Revolution brings communism to Russia.
1929	Worldwide economic depression begins.
1939	World War II begins, following the German invasion of Poland.
1945	World War II ends.
1957	The Vietnam War starts.
1969	Humans land on the moon.
1975	The Vietnam War ends.
1979	Soviet Union invades Afghanistan.
1983	Drought and famine in Africa.
1989	The Berlin Wall is torn down as communism crumbles in Eastern Europe.
1991	Soviet Union breaks into separate states.
1992	Bill Clinton is elected U.S. president.
2000	George W. Bush is elected U.S. president.
2001	Terrorists attack World Trade Center, New York, and the Pentagon, Washington, D.C.

Fast Facts

Official name: Hashemite Kingdom of Jordan

Capital: Amman

Official language: Arabic

Amman

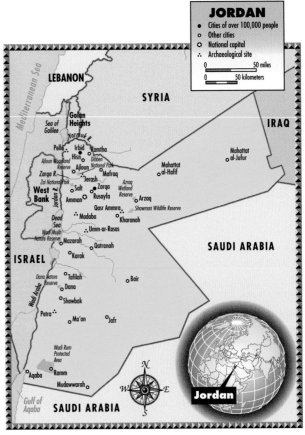

Jordan's flag

The Great Rift Valley

Official religion:	Islam
Year of founding:	1946
Founder:	King Abdullah I
National anthem:	"Asha al-Malik" ("Long Live the King")
Government:	Constitutional monarchy
Chief of state:	King
Head of government:	Prime minister
Area:	35,467 square miles (91,860 sq km)
Greatest distance north to south:	235 miles (378 km)
Greatest distance east to west:	225 miles (362 km)
Land and water borders:	Syria to the north; Iraq to the northeast; Saudi Arabia to the east and south; Gulf of Aqaba to the south; Israel, the West Bank, and the Dead Sea to the west
Highest elevation:	Jebel Rum, 5,755 feet (1,754 m) above sea level
Lowest elevation:	Shore of the Dead Sea, 1,339 feet (408 m) below sea level, the lowest point on Earth
Average temperature extremes:	100°F (38°C) in July near the Dead Sea and in the desert; 40°F (4°C) in January in the highlands
Average precipitation extremes:	Less than 2 inches (5 cm) in the desert; 25 inches (64 cm) in the northern highlands

Petra

Currency

**National population
(2005 est.):** 5,759,732

**Population of
largest cities:**

Amman	1,864,809
Zarqa	484,614
Irbid	313,121
Rusayfah	269,458
Aqaba	110,215

Famous landmarks:
- ▶ *Abu Darwish Mosque*, Amman
- ▶ *Dana Nature Reserve*
- ▶ *Dead Sea*
- ▶ *Petra*
- ▶ *Roman ruins*, Jerash
- ▶ *Shaumari Wildlife Reserve*, near Azraq

Industry: Potash, phosphates, and gypsum are Jordan's most important mineral products. Cement and refined petroleum are leading manufactured goods. Fertilizer, medicines, leather goods, textiles, and food products are other important Jordanian products.

Currency: The Jordanian dinar. In 2006, 1 Jordanian dinar equaled US$1.41.

**System of weights
and measures:** Metric system

Literacy rate: 91.3 percent

Bedouins

Common Arabic words and phrases:

'afwan	You're welcome
aysh ismak?	What's your name?
gadaysh se'aa?	What time is it?
gadaysh hada?	How much is it?
leh	No
keefak?	How are you?
ma assalaameh	Good-bye
marhaba	Hi
min fadlak	Please
naam	Yes
shukran	Thank-you

Famous Jordanians:

Abdullah I   (1882–1951)
First king of Jordan (1920–1951)

Abdullah II   (1962–)
King of Jordan (1999–present)

Hussein   (1935–1999)
Third king of Jordan (1953–1999)

Rania   (1970–)
Queen of Jordan (1999–present)

Mona Saudi   (1945–)
Sculptor

Mustafa Wahbi al-Tal   (1899–1949)
Poet

Hussein

To Find Out More

Nonfiction

▶ Carew-Miller, Anna. *Jordan*. Philadelphia: Mason Crest Publishers, 2004.

▶ Darraj, Susan Muaddi. *Queen Noor*. Philadelphia: Chelsea House Publishers, 2004.

▶ Wagner, Heather Lehr. *King Abdullah II*. Philadelphia: Chelsea House Publishers, 2005.

▶ Weintraub, Aileen. *The Dead Sea: The Saltiest Sea*. New York: PowerKids Press, 2001.

▶ Wills, Karen. *Jordan*. San Diego: Lucent Books, 2001.

Videos

▶ *The Hidden City of Petra*. New York: New Video Group, A&E Home Video, 1995. 50 minutes.

▶ *Jordan: The Royal Tour*. Bethesda, Md.: Check Six Productions for the Travel Channel, 2001. 52 minutes.

Web Sites

▶ **The Jordan Times**
http://www.jordantimes.com
The online version of Jordan's leading English-language daily newspaper.

▶ **Jordan Tourism Board**
http://www.see-jordan.com
*For information on Jordan's cities
and its historic and natural sites.*

▶ **King Abdullah II Official Web Site**
http://www.kingabdullah.jo
*The site includes a biography of the
king, news articles and press releases
about the king, official letters from and
speeches by the king, information about
the royal court and palaces, and the
history of modern Jordan.*

▶ **National Information System**
http://www.nic.gov.jo
*For information and statistics on
all areas of Jordanian life, including
agriculture, industry, geography, the
environment, population, and housing.*

▶ **Rania Al-Abdullah Queen
of Jordan**
http://www.queenrania.jo
*For all kinds of information about
the interests and official projects
of the queen.*

Organizations and Embassies

▶ **Jordan Embassy**
3504 International Drive NW
Washington, DC 20008
202-966-2664

▶ **Jordan Tourism Board
North America**
Courthouse Place
2000 North 14th Street, #770
Arlington, VA 22201
877-733-5673

Index

Page numbers in *italics* indicate illustrations.

Meet the Author

PATRICIA K. KUMMER writes and edits textbook materials and nonfiction books for children and young adults from her home office in Lisle, Illinois. She earned a bachelor's degree in history from the College of St. Catherine in St. Paul, Minnesota, and a master's degree in history from Marquette University in Milwaukee, Wisconsin. Before starting her career in publishing, she taught social studies at the junior high/middle school level.

Kummer has written biographies, books about the states, and books about American, African, Asian, and European history. Her books include *Cameroon*, *Côte d'Ivoire*, *Korea*, *Singapore*, *Syria*, *Tibet*, and *Ukraine* in the Children's Press Enchantment of the World series; and *The Calendar*, *Currency*, and *The Telephone* in the Franklin Watts series Inventions That Shaped the World. In addition to her writing, Ms. Kummer teaches a course about writing nonfiction books for children at the College of Du Page and serves as an elected trustee on the Lisle Library Board.

"Writing books about people, states, and countries requires a great deal of research," Kummer says. "My method of research begins by going online. There I compiled a list of the most recent books on Jordan. Many of the books were at my public library. For the books my library did not have, I placed interlibrary loan requests. I also interviewed Jordanian Americans who had recently visited Jordan about daily life in Jordan. In turn, these people gave me e-mail addresses of family and friends still living in Jordan. From them, I received current information about housing, family relationships, and the cost of many items. In addition, I found Web sites and news listservs that provided me with up-to-date information about the government and the economy."

Photo Credits

Photographs © 2007:

akg-Images, London: 110 (Ullstein Bild), 49 (National History Museum, Athens, Greece)

Alamy Images: 34 bottom, 58, 68, 71, 116 (Bill Lyons), 35 (Andrea Matone), 105 (Robert Harding Picture Library Ltd.), 60 (Terry Fincher Photo Int), 122 (TNT Magazine)

AP/Wide World Photos: 69 (Yousef Allan), 102 (Lefteris Pitarakis), 9 (Eyal Warshavsky)

Art Directors and TRIP Photo Library: 41 (Itzhak Genut), 15, 20, 38, 46, 70, 74 right, 76, 123, 131 bottom, 132 bottom (Helene Rogers), 22 (Adina Tovy), 120

Art Resource, NY/Erich Lessing/Israel Museum (IDAM), Jersualem, Israel: 43

Corbis Images: 25 bottom (Lynsey Addario), 24, 31 (Yann Arthus-Bertrand), 87 (Maher Attar/MGA Production), 39 (Dave Bartruff), 25 top (Annie Griffiths Belt), 50 (Bettmann), 84, 98 (Francoise de Mulder), 10, 133 bottom (Tim Graham), 99 (Peter Guttman), 33 (Chris Hellier), 12 (Jim Hollander/Reuters), 107 (Dave G. Houser/Post-Houserstock), 72 (Hanan Isachar), 7 bottom, 85, 92, 96, 109, 118 (Ali Jarekji/Reuters), 100 (Buddy Mays), 62 (Petra/Reuters), 104 (Carmen Redondo), 13 (Amit Shabi/Reuters), 75 (Moshe Shai), 55 (Peter Skingley/Bettmann), 54 (Leif Skoogfors), 19 bottom (Alison Wright)

Danita Delimont Stock Photography/Jon Arnold: 2

Dembinsky Photo Assoc./Claudia Adams: cover, 6, 125

Getty Images: 61 (AFP), 28 (Richard Ashworth/Robert Harding World Imagery), 114 (Joseph Barrak/AFP), 111 (Annie Griffiths Belt/National Geographic), 66, 130 left (Alistair Duncan/Dorling Kindersley), 57 (Thomas Hartwell/Time & Life Pictures), 83 (Chris Hondros), 93 (Khalil Mazraawi/AFP), 65 (Rabih Moghrabi/AFP), 81, 101 (Jamal Nasrallah/AFP), 95 (Jewel Samad/AFP), 103 (David Silverman)

Index Stock Imagery/Tina Buckman: 73

Landov, LLC/Jamal Nasrallah/EPA: 115

Larry Luxner: 23, 112

Lonely Planet Images: 7 top, 21, 30 bottom (Anders Blomqvist), 117 (Olivier Cirendini), 36, 37 (Mark Daffey), 19 top (John Elk III), 79 (Jean Robert)

Magnum Photos/Micha Bar Am: 27

MapQuest.com, Inc.: 59, 131 top

NHPA/Paul Brough: 34 top Panos Pictures: 126 (Yola Monakhov), 90 (Giacomo Pirozzi), 29 (Jon Spaull)

Peter Arnold Inc.: 74 left (BIOS), 119, 133 top (Lutz Jaekel/Bilderberg)

Photo Researchers, NY: 26, 30 top (David Hosking), 16 (Noboru Komine)

Superstock, Inc./age fotostock: 8, 89, 132 top

The Art Archive/Picture Desk/Dagli Orti: 40 (Musée du Louvre Paris), 47

The Image Works: 80 (Chet Gordon), 91, 124 (Richard Lord), 97 (Josef Polleross), 17 (Norbert Schiller), 51 (Topham), 108 (Alison Wright)

TIPS Images/Reinhard Dirscherl: 32

Wolfgang Kaehler: 45

Maps and Illustrations by XNR Productions, Inc.